The Global Flow of Aluminum From 2006 Through 2025

By W.D. Menzie, JJ Barry, D.I. Bleiwas, E.L. Bray, T.G. Goonan, and Grecia Matos

Open-File Report 2010–1256

U.S. Department of the Interior
U.S. Geological Survey

U.S. Department of the Interior
KEN SALAZAR, Secretary

U.S. Geological Survey
Marcia K. McNutt, Director

U.S. Geological Survey, Reston, Virginia: 2010

For more information on the USGS—the Federal source for science about the Earth,
its natural and living resources, natural hazards, and the environment—
visit *http://www.usgs.gov* or call 1–888–ASK–USGS.

For an overview of USGS information products, including maps, imagery, and publications,
visit *http://www.usgs.gov/pubprod*

To order this and other USGS information products, visit *http://store.usgs.gov*

Suggested citation:
Menzie, W.D., Barry, JJ, Bleiwas, D.I., Bray, E.L., Goonan, T.G., and Matos, Grecia, 2010, The global flow of
aluminum from 2006 through 2025: U.S. Geological Survey Open-File Report 2010–1256, 73 p., available at
http://pubs.usgs.gov/of/2010/1256/.

Contents

Figures

Tables

Conversion Factors

Multiply	By	To obtain
Length		
inch (in.)	2.54	centimeter (cm)
inch (in.)	25.4	millimeter (mm)
foot (ft)	0.3048	meter (m)
mile (mi)	1.609	kilometer (km)
Area		
acre	4,047	square meter (m^2)
square foot (ft^2)	0.09290	square meter (m^2)
square inch (in^2)	6.452	square centimeter (cm^2)
square mile (mi^2)	2.590	square kilometer (km^2)
Volume		
ounce, fluid (fl. oz)	0.02957	liter (L)
cubic inch (in^3)	16.39	cubic centimeter (cm^3)
cubic foot (ft^3)	0.02832	cubic meter (m^3)
Mass		
ounce, avoirdupois (oz)	28.35	gram (g)
pound, avoirdupois (lb)	0.4536	kilogram (kg)
ton, short (2,000 lb)	0.9072	megagram (Mg) or metric ton (t)
Energy		
foot-pound (ft·lb)	1.356	joule (J)
horsepower (HP)	746	watt (W)

Temperature in degrees Celsius (°C) may be converted to degrees Fahrenheit (°F) as follows:
$$°F = (1.8 \times °C) + 32.$$

The Global Flow of Aluminum From 2006 Through 2025

By W.D. Menzie, JJ Barry, D.I. Bleiwas, E.L. Bray, T.G. Goonan, and Grecia Matos

Executive Summary

This report presents results of an investigation of the global flow of materials related to the production and use of aluminum in 2006 and makes projections to 2025. The report was prepared in cooperation with the U.S. Environmental Protection Agency for the Organisation for Economic Co-operation and Development, Environmental Policy Committee's Working Group on Waste Prevention and Recycling. The report addresses the major resource flows and effects of those flows and provides insights on the life cycle of aluminum; it does not address policy issues related to the production and use of aluminum.

The report describes the flow of aluminum for 2006 at a macro level (country and global scales) based mainly on production data for bauxite, alumina, and aluminum gathered by the U.S. Geological Survey (USGS). Compared with findings from previous studies, this report estimates a similar level for the flow of primary aluminum (aluminum made from bauxite). The flow of secondary aluminum (aluminum made from fabrication and post-consumer scrap), however, is lower than that estimated by previous studies; this discrepancy should be further investigated.

The report also describes flows of materials associated with the production of primary and secondary aluminum at the micro level. These materials include both major inputs to bauxite, alumina, and aluminum production and outputs from that production. Outputs of significant environmental concern include red mud that is produced as a result of the production of alumina from bauxite, and greenhouse gases (including CO_2 from electricity generation and perfluorocarbons that are produced during electrolysis) that are produced as a result of the smelting of alumina to produce aluminum.

The consumption of aluminum by end-use category in high-income countries compared with that in low- to middle-income countries is analyzed. The leading use of aluminum in many high-income countries is to produce goods in the transportation sector. In low- to middle-income countries, aluminum is used mainly in the production of electrical systems and by the construction industry. Differences in the end uses of aluminum by income have important implications for the recovery of post-consumer scrap because the in-service life of electrical systems and construction uses is much longer than that of many transportation uses.

The report investigates the end uses of aluminum by the transportation sector in some detail. In particular, the report examines the use of aluminum in the manufacture of automobiles and commercial aircraft. Production of these goods generates different amounts of fabrication scrap and the goods have different in-service periods, which are two factors that are important to recovery of aluminum scrap.

Aluminum production and consumption may be considered as the two sides of a single coin for the purposes of materials flow analysis. Consequently, the report presents both short- and medium-term forecasts of aluminum production based on a USGS compilation of planned changes in bauxite and aluminum production capacity on a country-by-country basis and a long-term forecast (to 2025) of aluminum consumption based a new method of analyzing and projecting future aluminum flows. The method combines a model that predicts aluminum consumption from economic growth rates with information about changes in end-use consumption that occur with changes in income to forecast levels of aluminum consumption and to draw inferences about the availability of aluminum scrap.

Based upon announced production plans, the capacity of bauxite mines worldwide is expected to increase to 270 million metric tons (Mt) by 2015 from 183 Mt in 2006, or by almost 48 percent. Future aluminum production capacity based upon announced production plans is expected to reach 61 Mt in 2015 compared with 45.3 Mt in 2006, which is an increase of 35 percent, or almost 3.4 percent per year.

By 2025, aluminum consumption is likely to increase by more that 2.5 times to 120 Mt compared with 45.3 Mt in 2006. This represents a growth rate of 4.1 percent per year. Most of the increased consumption will take place in countries that consumed only modest amounts of aluminum in 2006. China, which consumed about 6.6 kilograms per capita in 2006, is expected to consume 28.7 kilograms per capita in 2025. Russia, Brazil, and India also are expected to increase their aluminum consumption significantly. Consumption in high-income countries is not expected to change significantly on a per capita basis, but total consumption may change modestly owing to changes in population.

To meet the projected consumption of 120 Mt of aluminum, the world would need to produce about 570 Mt of bauxite and about 230 Mt of alumina. This production will generate significant levels of waste even if technological improvements are made to current production processes.

A key question related to this projected increase in consumption is what portion of the consumption will be satisfied by primary aluminum and what portion will be sourced from secondary aluminum, as this will have a considerable influence on the amount of greenhouse gases generated by aluminum production. That portion of secondary aluminum that comes from new scrap is likely to increase proportionately with overall consumption. The data on changing patterns of end use that come with increased income, however, suggest that, at least initially, the proportion of aluminum that is generated from old scrap may decrease as countries undergoing economic growth initially use aluminum to develop new infrastructure, which has a long term of in-service use. Later, recycling of post-consumer scrap could increase.

If the proportion of aluminum production that comes from primary smelters increases, at least until 2025, a reduction in greehhouse gases from aluminum production must come from increases in the efficiency of aluminum smelters or from reduced use of fossil fuels to generate the electricity used in aluminum production.

1. Introduction

This study was undertaken at the request of the U.S. Environmental Protection Agency to support the Organisation for Economic Co-operation and Development, Environmental Policy Committee's Working Group on Waste Prevention and Recycling. The Working Group commissioned case studies of four different materials [wood fibers, plastics, critical metals (those used in electronics), and aluminum] to examine the role that materials flow studies might play in the development of policy to promote sustainable materials management. The Working Group identified four key questions it hopes to address through the case studies—

1. What are the major resource flows and environmental impacts and how are they expected to evolve in the future? To what extent is natural capital preserved?

2. How can new insights be gained and translated into new measures by taking a life cycle perspective? To what extent has it been possible to consider the complete materials life cycle?

3. What policy measures have been taken or can be taken to stimulate sustainable environmental, economic, and social outcomes?

4. To what extents are different actors in society engaged in taking up active ethically based responsibilities for sustainable outcomes?

This study of aluminum addresses the first two questions.

2. Background and Methods

2.1. Life Cycle of Aluminum

Aluminum is one of the most important metals used by modern societies. Aluminum's combination of physical properties results in its use in a wide variety of products, many of which are indispensable to modern life. Because of its light weight and electrical conductivity, aluminum wire is used for long-distance transmission of electricity. Aluminum's strength, light weight, and workability have led to increased use in transportation systems, including light vehicles, railcars, and aircraft, as efforts to reduce fuel consumption have increased. Aluminum's excellent thermal properties and resistance to corrosion have led to its use in air conditioning, refrigeration, and heat-exchange systems. Finally, its malleability has allowed it to be rolled and formed into very thin sheets used in a variety of packaging.

Figure 1 is a generalized model of the entire life cycle, or flow, of aluminum. Primary aluminum production begins with the mining of bauxite, which is processed first into alumina and subsequently into aluminum metal. The main wastes from bauxite mining are tailings produced by grinding and washing the bauxite. The processing of bauxite to alumina involves initial chemical processing of the bauxite. The main waste from alumina refining is the production of "red mud," a waste that is usually disposed of in a landfill. The electrolysis of alumina to produce aluminum involves the use of aluminum fluoride, carbon anodes, and large amounts of electricity. The most significant waste products from the production of aluminum from alumina are air emissions, including perfluorocarbon (PFC) gases and carbon dioxide (CO_2) from the production of anodes and electricity.

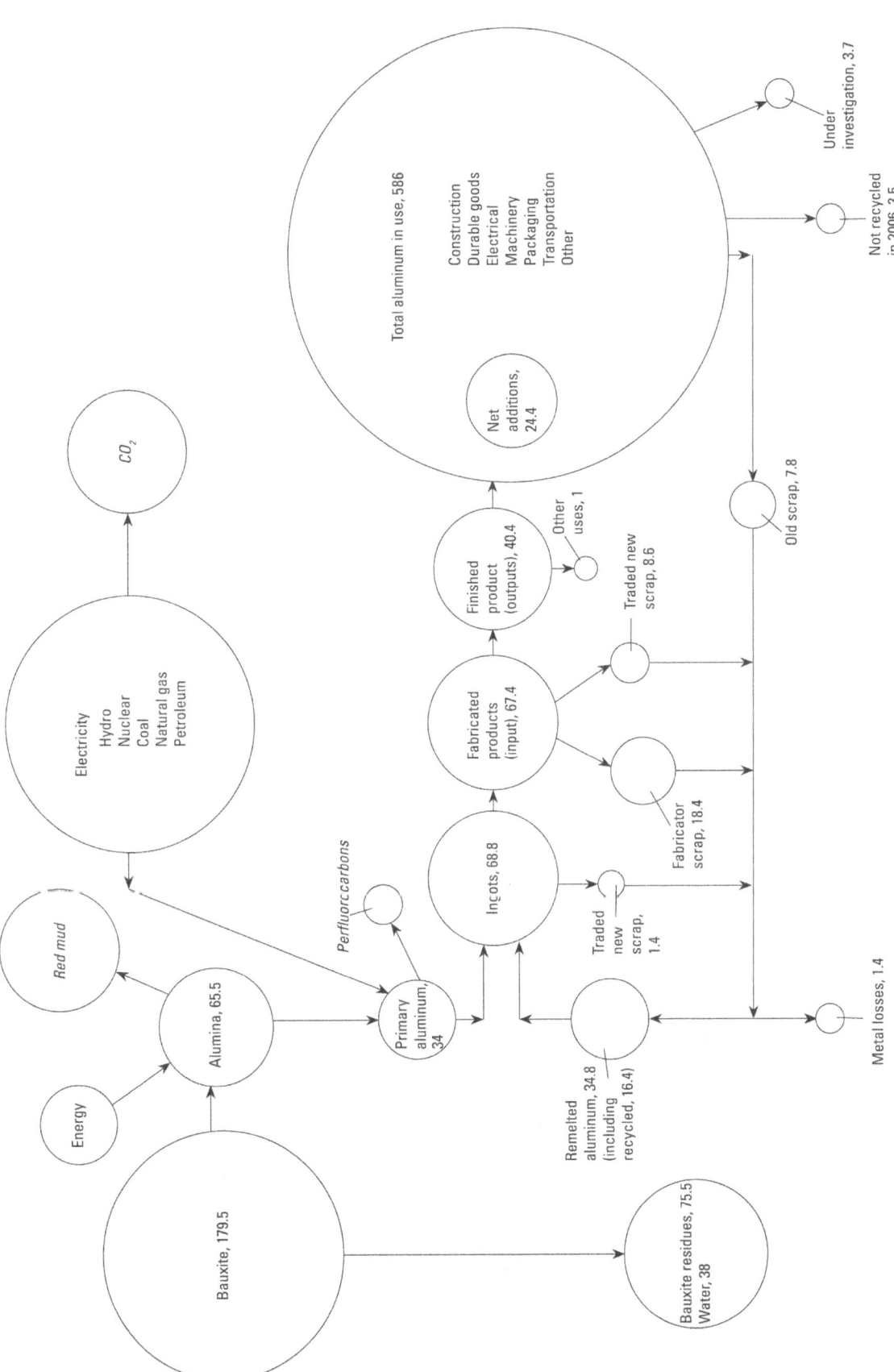

Figure 1. Diagram showing the global flow (life cycle) of aluminum in 2006. Data are in metric tons; emissions are in italics. Modified from Martchek (2007).

5

Following smelting of the alumina to produce aluminum, the metal is poured into several basic shapes. These shapes are then fabricated into semimanufactured goods and then processed into finished goods. Fabrication may involve rolling the metal into sheets, casting the metal into shapes, drawing the metal into wire, or extrusion of the metal to produce different shapes. The amount of waste, or scrap, from fabrication and manufacture varies, depending on individual processes. For example, cutting of aluminum sheet produces significant amounts of scrap whereas casting aluminum parts produces little scrap. Scrap from fabrication and the manufacture of finished goods is generally recycled and is called new scrap. The main end uses, or classes, of aluminum-bearing goods include buildings (construction), durable goods, electrical (power), machinery, packaging, and transportation. Old, or post-consumer, scrap is generated at various rates for different types of goods, depending on the in-service life of the goods and the economics of collecting and recovering aluminum from the good.

2.2. Previous Studies

The present report relies upon several seminal studies of U.S. and global aluminum flows. Martchek (2006) describes a model developed by Alcoa Inc. to provide estimates of the global aluminum flows and system losses from 1950 to 2003. Resource requirements and life cycle flows were estimated by combining aluminum flows with global average life cycle flow data developed from producers through the International Aluminium Institute (IAI). The model shows mass flows for primary and secondary (recycled) aluminum, including material from fabrication and manufacture of finished products; total aluminum in use; and three classes of losses (losses in recycling, material sent to landfills, and material under study). Recycled material is broken into four classes—aluminum skimmed in ingot production, internal scrap generated in the aluminum smelter, new scrap generated by fabricators, and old scrap generated by consumers of final goods. The amount of aluminum in the different types of scrap was estimated by teams of experts using statistical data and technical literature on aluminum production. The model used historic end-use data from regional aluminum associations to estimate future disposition of aluminum production. Martchek (2006) also presents data on past production of greenhouse gases (GHGs) and estimates of future GHG emissions from aluminum production that take into account increased use of recycled (secondary) aluminum and reductions in emissions in the production of primary aluminum.

Martchek (2007) presents updated estimates of global aluminum flows in 2006 and estimates of the amount of GHG emissions generated by the major steps leading to the production of aluminum ingot. IAI presents updated (2005) life cycle data for primary aluminum, including raw materials and energy use, air and water emissions, and solid wastes generated (International Aluminium Institute, 2007).

In recent years, numerous reports on the flow of metals have appeared in the technical literature (see, for example, reports by Graedel and his colleagues at the Center for Industrial Ecology at Yale University). Two reports that are applicable to aluminum flows include those of Hatayama and others (2007) and Chen and others (2009).

2.3. Methods of Present Study

The method developed for the Alcoa and IAI studies require some data and capabilities that were not available for the present study. In particular, this study lacked long-term data on end uses of aluminum in different regions, data on the flow within smelters, and the availability of experts who could estimate recycling rates. These deficiencies placed constraints on the study and required the development of an alternative method to estimate present and future aluminum flows. This study used data for 2006 so that flows common to this study and the IAI model can be compared and so more detailed flows from the Alcoa and IAI studies can be used with this study to obtain a more complete picture of flows associated with aluminum production and use.

The forecast in the present study is based on a model that relates resource consumption (use) to average national income as measured by gross domestic product (GDP) per capita. Previous studies (DeYoung and Menzie, 1999; Menzie, DeYoung, and Steblez, 2001) have shown that industrial consumption of such metals as copper and aluminum is low at low levels of income and high but stable once a threshold income is reached. As countries increase their per capita income, industrial consumption increases rapidly until the threshold is reached. Previous studies also show that the 20 most populous countries typically consume about 70 percent of global production. As a result, this study focuses on high-income populous countries and selected populous countries experiencing rapid economic growth.

This study summarizes global (macro-level) aluminum mass flows in terms of the production of bauxite, alumina, and primary and secondary aluminum, and the apparent consumption of aluminum. All production data, except the estimated secondary aluminum production for Russia, are taken from the aluminum chapter (Bray, 2010a) of volume I of the USGS Minerals Yearbook (MYB) and various country chapters of volume III of the MYB. An estimate of Russia's secondary aluminum production was made based upon Grishayev and Petrov (2008). Consumption data were taken from various publications of the World Bureau of Metal Statistics (*www.world-bureau.com*) or were calculated from USGS production data and trade data from the United Nations Comtrade database (*comtrade.un.org*).

Micro-level flows of materials associated with the production of primary aluminum are presented as a model of materials inputs to and outputs from the production of primary aluminum from bauxite; the model, which was developed by Goonan and Bleiwas, is based upon input and output data from the IAI and the European Aluminium Association (EAA). The model consists of the following three submodels: (1) a model of the inputs to and outputs from bauxite mining, (2) a model of alumina production, and (3) a model of primary aluminum production. The alumina and primary aluminum models cover two cases—a model of world plants and a model of European plants. An additional model examines the inputs to and outputs from the secondary aluminum production process. These models are used to estimate inputs to and outputs from various parts of the bauxite to alumina to aluminum production process and the aluminum remelt production process.

Aluminum consumption per capita and the end uses of aluminum were examined for the following high-income countries and low- and middle-income countries with rapidly growing economies—Argentina, Brazil, China, France, Germany, India, Japan, Mexico, Russia, the United Kingdom, and the United States. End-use data are reported for different classes for different countries. In spite of differences in classification, the end-use data suggest some broad changes in the end uses of aluminum as income increases. The end-use statistics have been compared with light vehicle manufacturing and vehicle aluminum intensity data (Ducker Worldwide LLC, 2008, p. 38) to further specify the use of aluminum. Data on commercial aircraft production and weight were collected for four important aircraft manufacturers—Airbus, Boeing, Bombardier, and Embraer. An estimate that 80 percent of the weight of an aircraft is aluminum was used with these data to estimate the aluminum in use in commercial aircraft. For vehicles and aircraft, scrap that was generated in the process of manufacture was estimated.

Future mass flows of aluminum are estimated by two methods. Short- to medium-term (2008 to 2015) flows were estimated using aluminum outlooks published in the regional summary chapters of volume III of the MYB (Fong-Sam and others, 2009, p. 1.17; Anderson and others, 2010, p. 1.27; Levine and others, 2010, p. 1.35; Mobbs and others, 2010, p. 1.9; Yager and others, 2010, p. 1.18). The outlooks are compilations based upon industry announcements of new or expanded plant capacity.

Longer-term flows are estimated using a logistic regression linking aluminum consumption per capita to GDP per capita, which is a measure of income. The model uses the logistic regression, population growth rates, and 10-year forecasts of economic growth for each of the 20 most populous countries to estimate future consumption. Estimates of aluminum consumption are combined with the models of materials inputs and outputs to make status quo estimates of material requirements and the wastes generated.

3. Findings

3.1. Global Mass Flows of Aluminum

This report considers material flows related to the production, use, and recycling of aluminum at the macro and micro levels. The macro-level flows include the production from bauxite, alumina, and primary aluminum; the consumption of aluminum by end-use; and the production of secondary aluminum. Micro-level flows of materials associated with the production of primary and secondary aluminum include the inputs to and outputs from the production of bauxite, alumina, primary aluminum, and secondary aluminum. These flows are presented in terms of 1 metric ton (t) of output of each product. Environmental issues related to the production of each product are discussed in terms of the outputs that result in the issue.

3.1.1. Macro-Level Flows of Aluminum—Production

Production data on bauxite, alumina, and primary and secondary aluminum production are in tables 1 through 3, respectively. Data on the location, ownership, and production capacity of the majority of the bauxite, alumina, and aluminum production facilities are in appendixes 1 through 3, respectively. For most facilities, appendixes 1 through 3 reflect their characteristics in 2007.

3.1.1.1. Bauxite

Based upon data in volumes I and III of the MYB, just over 183 million metric tons (Mt) of bauxite was produced in 2006; of this amount, 50 Mt was produced in the Americas; 104 Mt, in Asia; 9.6 Mt, in Europe and Eurasia; and 18.8 Mt, in Africa and the Middle East. Six countries each produced more than 10 Mt of bauxite (Australia, 61.8 Mt; China, 27 Mt; Brazil, 22.8 Mt; Guinea, 16.3 Mt; Jamaica, 14.9 Mt; and India, 13.9 Mt) and together accounted for 85 percent of global production. The distribution of bauxite production reflects the geologic history and climatic factors that favor the formation of bauxite as well as economic factors, such as the cost of production at individual sites.

9

Table 1. Global production of bauxite in 2006.

[Data are from USGS Minerals Yearbook 2007, v. I and III]

Region and country	Quantity, in metric tons
Americas:	
Brazil	22,836,000
Guyana	1,479,000
Jamaica	14,865,000
Suriname	4,924,000
Venezuela	5,928,000
Total	50,032,000
Asia:	
Australia	61,780,000
China	27,000,000
India	13,940,000
Indonesia	1,502,000
Malaysia	92,000
Pakistan	7,000
Vietnam	30,000
Total	104,351,000
Europe and Eurasia:	
Bosnia and Herzegovina	854,000
France	168,000
Greece	2,163,000
Hungry	538,000
Kazakhstan	4,860,000
Russia	1,000,000
Total	9,583,000
Africa and the Middle East:	
Ghana	886,000
Guinea	16,300,000
Iran	500,000
Mozambique	11,000
Sierra Leone	1,072,000
Tanzania	5,000
Total	18,774,000
World total	182,740,000

3.1.1.2. Alumina

Global alumina production in 2006 was 74 Mt; of this amount, 20.9 Mt was produced in the Americas; 35.1 Mt, in Asia; 16.2 Mt, in Europe and Eurasia; and 0.8 Mt, in Africa and the Middle East. Six countries produced more than 4 Mt of alumina—Australia, 18.3 Mt; China, 13.7 Mt; Brazil, 6.8 Mt; Russia, 6.4 Mt; the United States, 4.7 Mt; and Jamaica, 4.1 Mt—and they accounted for about 72 percent of global alumina production. Not all alumina is used to produce aluminum; about 10 percent of alumina is used to produce refractory and other chemical products. Thus, about 67 Mt of alumina was available for aluminum production. That four of the six leading alumina producers are also among the six leading bauxite producers follows from the transportation advantage obtained by colocating alumina production facilities near bauxite mines and thereby avoiding the cost of transporting the waste material associated with the bauxite.

Table 2. Global production of alumina in 2006.

[Data are from USGS Minerals Yearbook 2007, v. I and III]

Region and country	Quantity, in metric tons
Americas:	
Brazil	6,793,000
Canada	1,281,000
Jamaica	4,100,000
Suriname	2,153,000
United States	4,700,000
Venezuela	1,892,000
Total	20,919,000
Asia:	
Australia	18,312,000
China	13,700,000
India	2,800,000
Japan	330,000
Total	35,142,000
Europe and Eurasia:	
Azerbaijan	363,000
Bosnia and Herzegovina	394,000
France	200,000
Germany	850,000
Greece	775,000
Hungry	270,000
Ireland	1,800,000
Italy	1,090,000
Kazakhstan	1,515,000
Montenegro	237,000
Romania	622,000
Russia	6,399,000
Spain	1,000,000
Ukraine	1,672,000
Total	16,187,000
Africa and the Middle East:	
Guinea	545,000
Iran	250,000
Total	795,000
World total	73,043,000

3.1.1.3. Aluminum

Global production of aluminum in 2006 was about 45.9 Mt; 34 Mt was primary aluminum produced by processing bauxite to alumina and then smelting the alumina to produce aluminum, and 11.8 Mt was secondary aluminum that was recovered from new scrap generated in the aluminum production process and old or post-consumer scrap. The Americas produced 7.82 Mt of primary aluminum; Asia, 13.0 Mt; Europe and Eurasia, 9.4 Mt; and Africa and the Middle East, 3.86 Mt. Eight countries produced at least 1 Mt of primary aluminum—China, 9.36 Mt; Russia, 3.72 Mt; Canada, 3.05 Mt; the United States, 2.28 Mt; Australia ,1.93 Mt; Brazil, 1.61 Mt; Norway, 1.42 Mt; and India, 1.10 Mt. Together, these eight countries accounted for about 72 percent of global primary aluminum production. Five of the six leading producers of primary aluminum were also among the six leading producers of alumina. Canada, which does not produce bauxite and was not one of the six leading producers of alumina, was the third ranked producer of primary aluminum. Abundant hydroelectricity led to the location of aluminum smelters in Canada. Aluminum smelting is energy intensive, and changes in the price and availability of energy result in the location of new smelters in areas with cheap and available energy. The availability of abundant supplies of natural gas has led to the development of significant aluminum smelters in Bahrain and the United Arab Emirates in recent years. Both countries produced more than 850,000 t of aluminum in 2006. New aluminum smelters are being built in Iceland, such as the Fjardaal smelter, because of the availability of abundant electricity generated from hydropower and geothermal power. The imposition of carbon taxes or carbon emissions pricing could significantly affect the location of aluminum smelters as companies move facilities to countries with abundant, cheaper energy. The closure of several aluminum smelters in the United States in recent years has been, in large part, a response to increased energy costs.

Of the secondary aluminum output, the Americas produced 4.46 Mt; Asia, 3.57 Mt; and Europe and Eurasia, 3.77 Mt. Production of secondary aluminum in Africa and the Middle East was negligible. Based upon USGS data, the six leading producers of secondary aluminum in 2006 accounted for 79 percent of global production of secondary aluminum. The United States produced 3.54 Mt; China, 2.35 Mt; Japan, 1.07 Mt; Germany, 0.8 Mt; Italy, 0.66 Mt; and Mexico, 0.6 Mt.

Data on global aluminum flows for 2006 are shown in figure 1, which is modified from Martchek (2007). The main modification has been in the end-use classes; the classes used in figure 1 correspond to USGS usage and contains the classes—construction, durable goods, electrical (power), machinery, packaging, transportation, and other. The classes used in Martchek (2007) follow European usage—building, engineering and cable, packaging, transportation, and other. Some countries keep a separate class for fabricated metal, which includes aluminum used in steelmaking. The classes electrical and machinery are particularly important for accounting for aluminum use in countries that are building infrastructure and developing a manufacturing sector.

Figure 1 shows global bauxite production inflows in 2006 as 179.5 Mt, which is very similar to the USGS estimate of 183.5 Mt, and calculates alumina flows as 65.5 Mt compared with the 67 Mt estimated in section 3.1.1.2. Figure 1 also shows primary metal production of 34 Mt, which is essentially the same as the production statistics in the MYB. Figure 1 also shows flows of 34.8 Mt of recovered metal, 18.4 Mt from metal recovered as scrap from fabrication operations, 8.6 Mt recovered from losses during the process of manufacturing goods, and 7.8 Mt of material collected after use by consumers. The 18.4 Mt of material "recycled" within the smelter facilities does not get counted in government statistics, and many governments do not separately report material recycled from the processes of manufacturing goods and material recovered after its use by consumers. The total amount of material recovered from both manufacturing and post-consumer use, identified as secondary aluminum in government statistics, is estimated to be 16.4 Mt by the IAI but 11.8 Mt by the USGS. The IAI data suggest that almost one-half of secondary aluminum is from post-consumer material. Statistics on secondary aluminum production in the United States indicate that 35 percent of secondary aluminum comes from post-consumer material (Papp, 2009, p. 61.2). All secondary aluminum reported for members of the European Union (EU27), the European Free Trade Association (EFTA), and Japan together with the old scrap (post-consumer) portion of secondary aluminum for the United States amounts to only 5.4 Mt of material. Clearly, efforts to harmonize these data are warranted.

Table 3. Global production of primary and secondary aluminum in 2006.

[NA, not available. Data are from USGS Minerals Yearbook 2007, v. I and III]

Region and country	Primary, in metric tons	Secondary, in metric tons
Americas:		
Argentina	273,000	16,000
Brazil	1,605,000	253,000
Canada	3,051,000	47,000
Mexico	NA	600,000
Venezuela	610,000	NA
United States	2,284,000	3,540,000
Total	7,823,000	4,456,000
Asia:		
Australia	1,932,000	130,000
China	9,360,000	2,350,000
India	1,104,000	NA
Indonesia	250,000	NA
Japan	57,000	1,070,000
New Zealand	337,000	22,000
Total	13,040,000	3,572,000
Europe and Eurasia:		
Austria	NA	150,000
Azerbaijan	32,000	NA
Bosnia and Herzegovina	136,000	NA
Bulgaria	NA	13,000
Croatia	NA	2,000
Czech Republic	NA	15,000
Denmark	NA	25,000
Finland	NA	36,000
France	442,000	222,000
Germany	516,000	796,000
Greece	165,000	3,000
Hungary	34,000	50,000
Iceland	328,000	NA
Italy	194,000	666,000
Montenegro	123,000	NA
Netherlands	312,000	25,000
Norway	1,422,000	349,000
Poland	58,000	19,000
Portugal	NA	18,000
Romania	267,000	11,000
Russia	3,718,000	550,000
Serbia	NA	1,000
Slovakia	161,000	NA
Slovenia	118,000	20,000
Spain	349,000	243,000
Sweden	101,000	32,000

Table 3. Global production of primary and secondary aluminum in 2006.—Continued

[NA, not available. Data are from USGS Minerals Yearbook 2007, v. I and III]

Region and country	Primary, in metric tons	Secondary, in metric tons
Europe and Eurasia—Continued:		
Switzerland	40,000	190,000
Tajikistan	414,000	NA
Ukraine	113,000	130,000
United Kingdom	360,000	198,000
Uzbekistan	NA	3,000
Total	9,403,000	3,767,000
Africa and the Middle East:		
Bahrain	860,000	NA
Cameroon	87,000	NA
Egypt	252,000	NA
Ghana	80,000	NA
Iran	205,000	NA
Kenya	NA	2,400
Mozambique	564,000	NA
South Africa	895,000	NA
Turkey	60,000	NA
United Arab Emirates	861,000	NA
Total	3,864,000	2,400
World total	34,130,000	11,797,000

3.1.2. Micro-Level Flows of Materials Associated with Aluminum Production

The preceding section of this paper addresses macro-level flows of aluminum to understand the production of aluminum goods and associated manufacturing wastes (primary scrap) and the generation of post-consumer wastes or scrap. This section of the paper focuses on the materials required to produce aluminum and the wastes generated in the production process; it is excerpted and modified from a draft manuscript by Goonan and Bleiwas, which presents models of the inputs to and outputs from the production of alumina from bauxite and of primary aluminum from alumina.

The IAI, the EAA, and others have been developing information on part of the aluminum life cycle through an Aluminum Sector Addendum, which addresses the Greenhouse Gas Protocol (for accounting and reporting) developed by the World Business Council for Sustainable Development in concert with the World Resources Institute. The IAI and EAA reports are the primary data sources for the information presented here.

The materials flows discussed in the sections that follow cover the primary production of aluminum, including bauxite mining (open pit), alumina production (Bayer process) and electrolytic smelting (Hall-Héroult process), and the production of secondary aluminum. Materials flow data in this report are taken from a 2008 report by the EAA, which developed two models (one for European plants and another for plants worldwide) for the various steps of the process to produce aluminum from bauxite. This report provides information about the steps used in primary aluminum production and is addressed to those interested in the generation of GHGs, red mud, and other effluvia associated with primary aluminum production. The inclusion of two models allows for the comparison of reductions in wastes that may be achieved just from adopting currently available technologies on a wider basis. Other opportunities for reducing air emissions by adopting enhanced technologies are discussed later in this section.

3.1.2.1. Bauxite Mining

The aluminum industry consumes nearly 90 percent of the bauxite mined; the remainder is used in abrasives, cement, ceramics, chemicals, metallurgical flux, refractory products, and miscellaneous products (Bray, 2010b). There are three main types of bauxite ore. They include trihydrate, which consists chiefly of gibbsite, $Al_2O_3 \cdot 3H_2O$; monohydrate, which consists mainly of boehmite, $Al_2O_3 \cdot H_2O$; and mixed bauxite, which consists of gibbsite and boehmite. The proportion of trihydrate and monohydrate ores in this type of bauxite differs from deposit to deposit as do the type and amount of impurities, such as clay, iron oxide, silica, and titania. Clay, free silica, iron hydroxide, and silt are also common constituents of bauxite ore. The alumina content of bauxite ores ranges from 31 to 52 percent, averaging about 41 percent on a production-weighted basis (International Aluminium Institute, 2009b). This study addresses the flow of metallurgical-grade bauxite ores used to produce aluminum. These ores typically have a minimum Al_2O_3 content of 50 to 55 percent with a texture that ranges from powdery clay to indurated (hardened by cementation) masses.

Bauxite mining operations generally require a large support network, which often requires significant capital and operating costs. The great majority of the world's bauxite ores are extracted by open-cut methods. Before mining of the ores can commence, it is usually necessary to remove overburden and to preserve the topsoil for post-mining rehabilitation. Most mines require the removal of 1 or 2 meters (m) of overburden (International Aluminium Institute, 2009b; Royal Boskalis Westminster NV, 2010). Bauxite ore bodies vary from 2 to 20 m in thickness (International Aluminium Institute, 2009b). The aerial extent can be highly variable.

Diesel-powered bulldozers, backhoes, front-end loaders, excavators, and haulage trucks are the principal tools used to remove and haul overburden and ore. The amount of equipment and the size of the equipment are dictated to a large extent by the mining environment (wet or dry, for example), stripping ratio, scale of production or capacity, and distance to shipment points. Additional equipment and materials required for the mining operation include roads, support vehicles, repair facilities, town site (houses, hospital, schools, and so forth), energy and freshwater production and distribution, communication systems, parts, and supplies. Rail and port facilities may be necessary, depending upon the location of the mine.

Some bauxite ores can be shipped directly to an alumina refinery without treatment because they are of sufficient grade and purity. Other ores may require added steps, such as size reduction and moisture content reduction prior to shipping. At some sites, the ore grade may be increased by removal of clays and other impurities by washing, wet screening, cycloning, and (or) sorting. Flotation is sometimes used to reduce the silica content of an ore. Blending of ores may also be used to maintain grade uniformity to meet specifications. Wastes (mostly clays) produced from processing are transported to and stored in tailings ponds. Ore that is to be transported appreciable distances to refineries is often dried to reduce shipping costs.

A small open pit bauxite mine may have an annual capacity of roughly 500,000 t of ore whereas the annual capacity of the largest mines approximates 23 Mt. Annual capacities of 3 Mt to 15 Mt of ore characterize most of the world's open pit bauxite operations. Bauxite mines operate for long periods of time; some as long as 100 years or more. Presently, the amount of land being opened for new or expanded bauxite mining equals the amount of post-mining land being rehabilitated, such that the total land use for bauxite mining worldwide would equal approximately one-half of the land area of Manhattan Island (New York City). The greatest difference between pre- and post-mining land use is a tradeoff between farming (11 to 12 percent) and native forest (49 to 60 percent) (International Aluminium Institute, 2009b). Figure 2, which shows the bauxite mining process flow, is based on a description of bauxite mining at the Alcoa-owned Juruti Mine in Brazil (Alcoa Inc., 2009).

The EAA has modeled the typical world bauxite mine. Figure 3 shows the generalized materials flows associated with world bauxite mining (European Aluminium Association, 2008). Inputs and outputs per metric ton of bauxite mined are measured in kilograms (gross), metric tons (gross), and cubic meters. The model presented in figure 3 does not include materials included in overburden or mine waste.

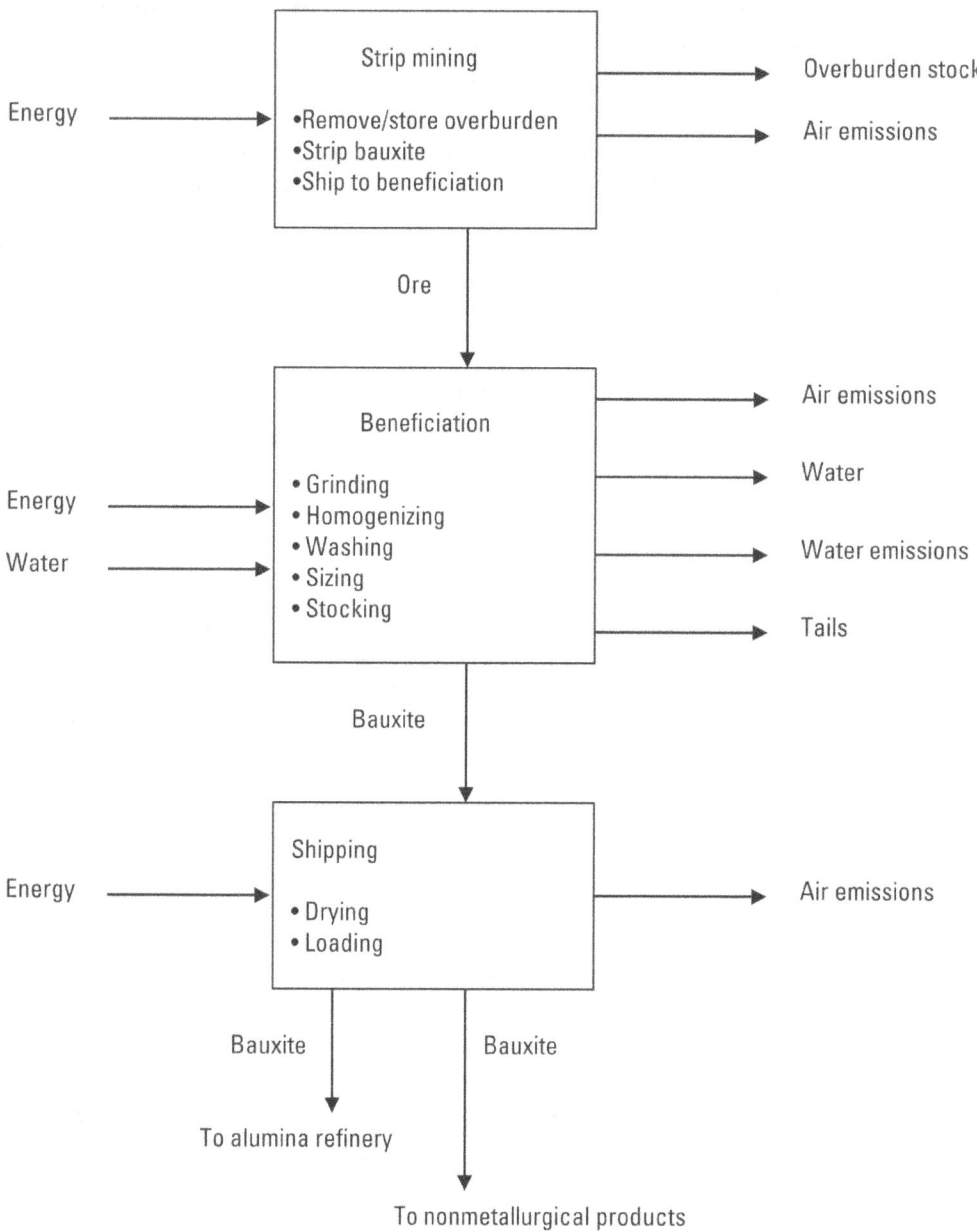

Figure 2.   Diagram showing a typical process flow for bauxite mining. Data are from Alcoa Inc. (2009).

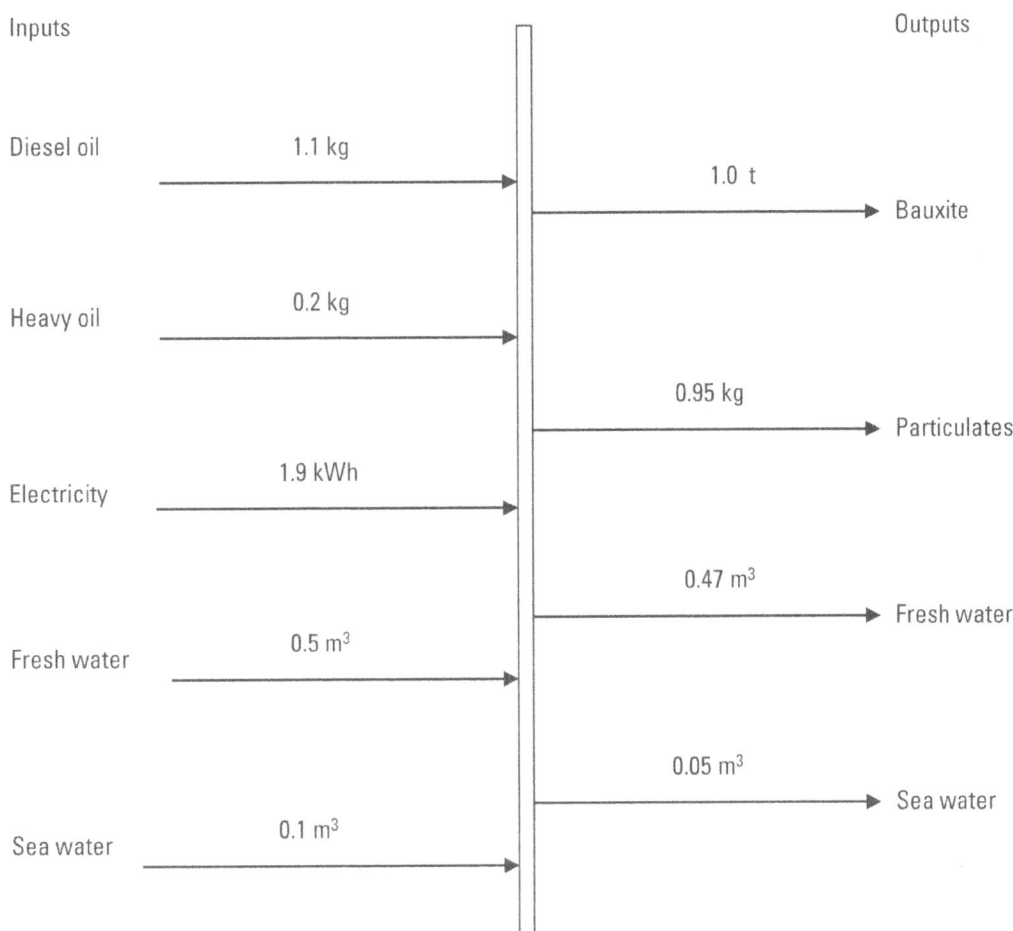

Inputs

Outputs

Diesel oil   1.1 kg

1.0 t
Bauxite

Heavy oil   0.2 kg

0.95 kg
Particulates

Electricity   1.9 kWh

0.47 m³
Fresh water

Fresh water   0.5 m³

0.05 m³
Sea water

Sea water   0.1 m³

Figure 3. Diagram showing selected materials flows for a World bauxite mine model. Data are from European Aluminium Association (2008, p. 23). kg, kilogram; kWh, kilowatthour; m³, cubic meter; t, metric ton.

3.1.2.2. Alumina Production (Refining)

Virtually all alumina commercially produced from bauxite is obtained by a process patented by Karl Josef Bayer (Austria) in 1888. The Bayer process involves the following steps:

- *Digestion.*—Bauxite is ground and slurried into a caustic soda (NaOH), which is then pumped into large pressure tanks called digesters. The sodium hydroxide reacts with the alumina minerals to form soluble sodium aluminate (NaAlOH).

- *Clarification.*—The solution from the digestion step is depressurized and processed through cyclones to remove coarse sand. The remaining fluid is processed in thickeners where flocculants are added to agglomerate solids, which are removed by cloth filters. These residues (red mud) are washed, combined, and discarded, and the clarified solution (containing the NaAlOH) is passed to the next step.

- *Precipitation.*—The solution from the clarification step is seeded with alumina seed (very small) crystals to aid precipitation of larger agglomerated alumina crystals. The product-sized crystals are separated from the small crystals (recycled as seed) and are washed to remove entrained caustic residue. The agglomerates are moved to the next step.

- *Calcination.*—The agglomerates of NaAlOH are placed in rotary kilns or stationary fluidized-bed calciners at temperatures that can exceed 960°C (1,750 °F), which drives off the chemically combined water, leaving a residue of commercial-grade alumina (Plunkert, 2006; Pontikes, 2005a).

Figure 4 shows the process flow for alumina refining (CiDRA Minerals Processing, Inc., 2010).

Materials flows within the Bayer process are dependent on the grade of the bauxite being processed and the amount and character of the nonalumina minerals contained in the bauxite. Figure 5 shows selected materials flows for a model "European" and "World" alumina refinery in 2005 (European Aluminium Association, 2008).

Figure 5 presents the inputs to and outputs from alumina production per metric ton of alumina as kilograms (gross), metric tons (gross), and cubic meters of the various materials. In 2005, the amount of bauxite required for a model European and World alumina refinery to produce 1 t of alumina was 2.2 t and 2.7 t, respectively, which indicates that, on average, European smelters were processing higher grade bauxite than the rest of the world. Red mud production from these models followed this trend reciprocally—that is, 706 kilograms per metric ton (kg/t) for the European model, and 1,142 kg/t for the World model (European Aluminium Association, 2008). Reduction of red mud waste by processing higher grade bauxite is not likely to represent a strategy for long-term sustainable production of aluminum because average grades of metals produced typically decline with time, as higher grade deposits are produced before lower grade ones.

The most important output from the Bayer process after alumina is red mud. The composition of red mud worldwide varies as follows: Fe_2O_3, 30 to 60 percent; Al_2O_3, 10 to 20 percent; SiO_2, 3 to 50 percent; Na_2O, 2 to 10 percent; CaO, 2 to 8 percent; and TiO_2, trace to 25 percent. Red mud is a highly complex material and its ultimate chemistry depends on the nature of the original bauxite ore. It is highly alkaline and contains a variety of elements and mineral species in small sizes and contains as much as 50 percent water (Pontikes, 2005b).

In the past, red mud has been disposed of at sea or contained in lined lake-size containment compounds (Pontikes, 2005c). While these practices still are used, research is ongoing to find better ways to recycle and reuse red mud—for example, as building materials (bricks, and roofing and flooring tiles), catalysts, ceramics, fillers, fertilizers, lightweight aggregates, metallurgical fluxes, and in the recovery of other metals (Pontikes, 2005d–e). In 2008, alumina refining worldwide produced about 93.2 Mt of red mud, of which 83.9 Mt was attributable to aluminum production. The reuse of red mud offers an opportunity to develop new industries based upon the wastes from alumina production.

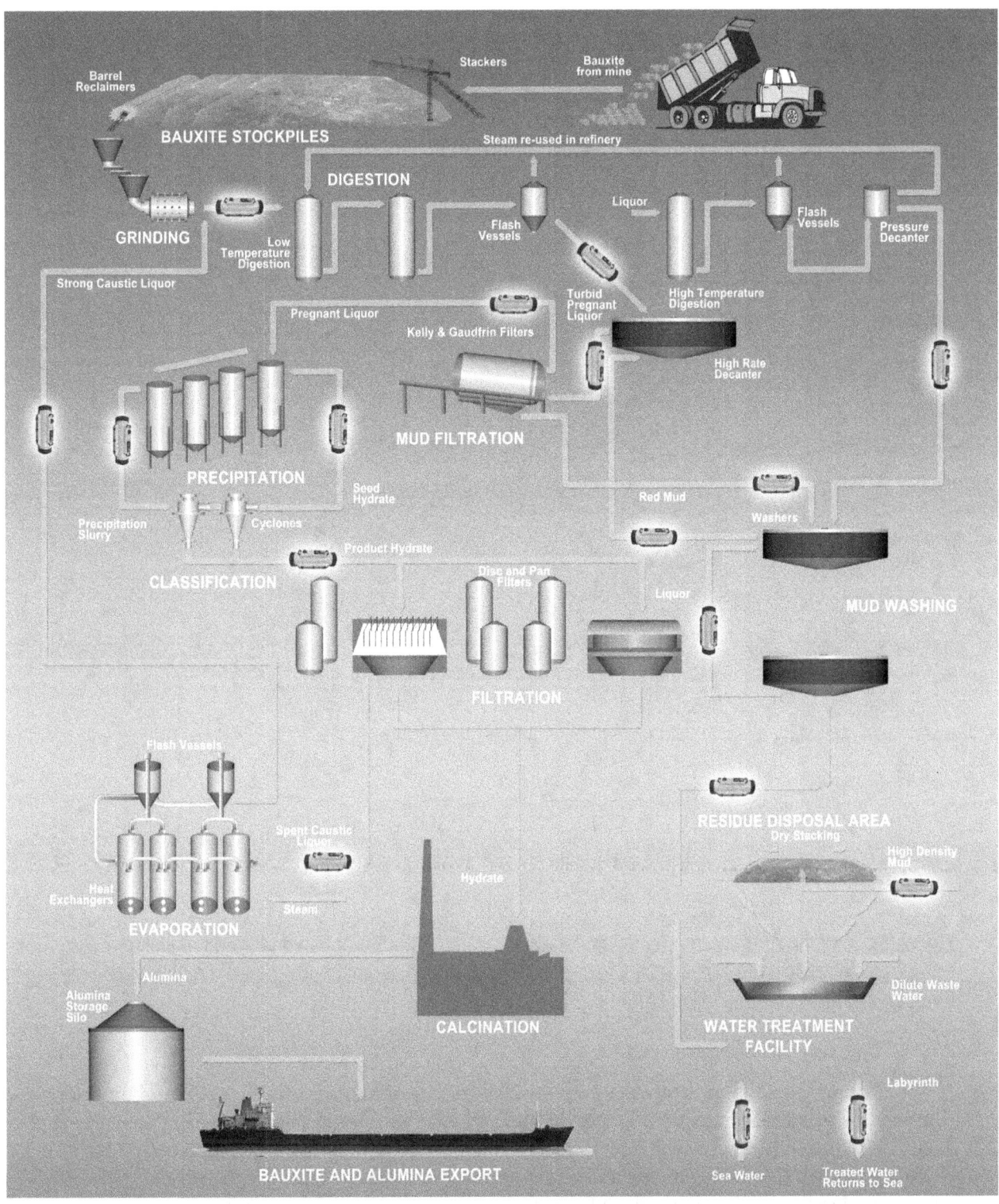

Figure 4. Diagram showing a typical process flow for alumina refining. From CIDRA Minerals Processing, Inc. (2010), used with permission.

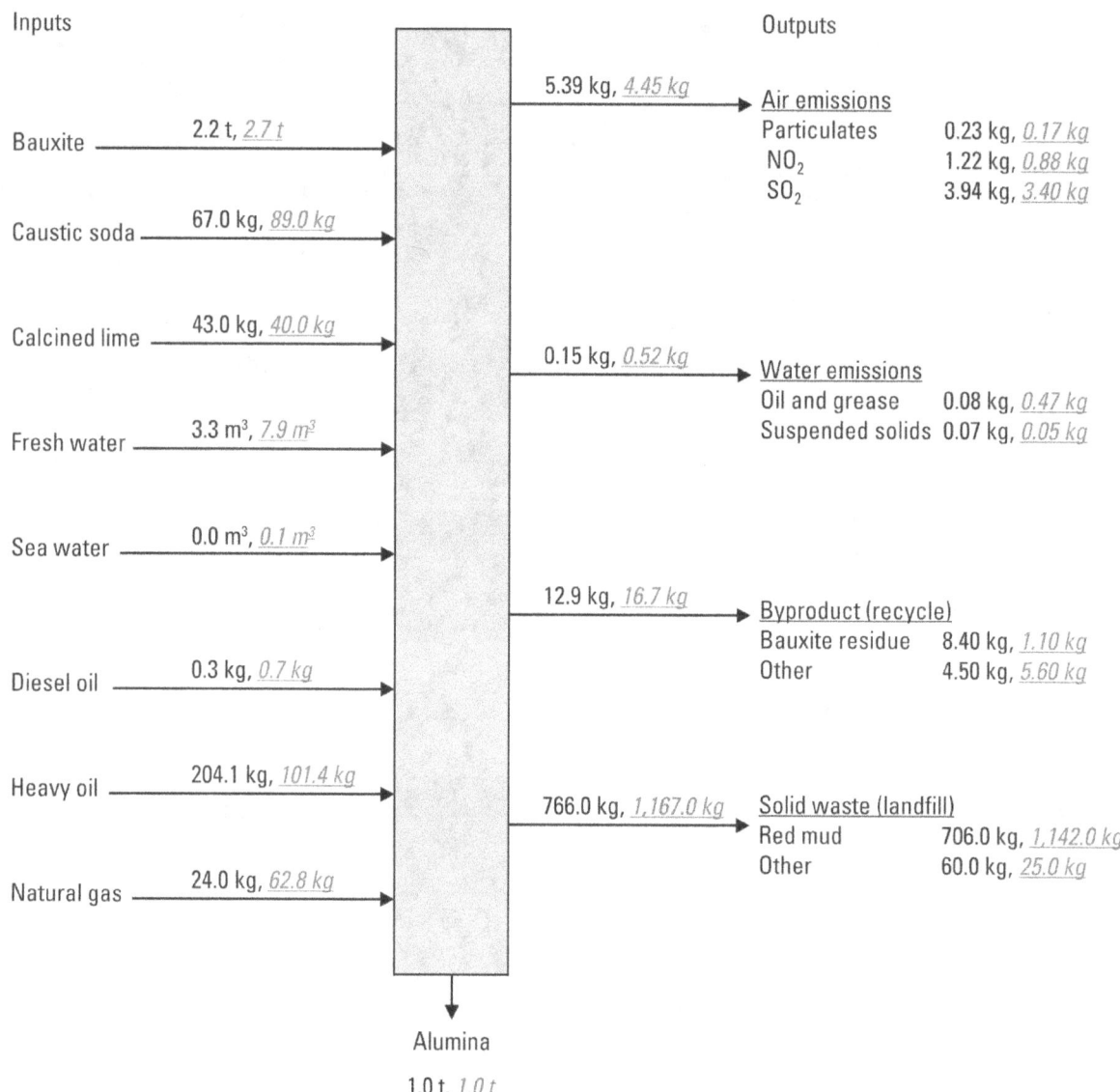

Figure 5. Diagram showing selected materials flows under the European and World alumina refinery models. European model data are in plain black text, and World model data are in underlined red italic text. Data are from European Aluminium Association (2008, p. 24).

3.1.2.3. Aluminum Smelting and Electrolysis

      Primary aluminum is produced by the electrolysis of alumina dissolved in molten fluoride salt. The process was independently invented in 1886 by Charles Martin Hall (United States) and Paul Louis Toussaint Héroult (France) and underwent continual improvement over the years. In the Hall-Héroult electrolytic reduction cell, alumina and aluminum fluoride are the material feedstocks. The carbon in anodes, which are either prebaked (in 90 percent of operations) or Söderberg-type (in 10 percent of operations), are consumed by reaction with the oxygen in the alumina to form carbon dioxide, which is ultimately released to the atmosphere. Figure 6 shows the process flows for aluminum smelting (Beck, 2008; European Aluminium Association, 2008). Ancillary to the aluminum reduction cell process is anode manufacturing, which generates additional emissions of concern.

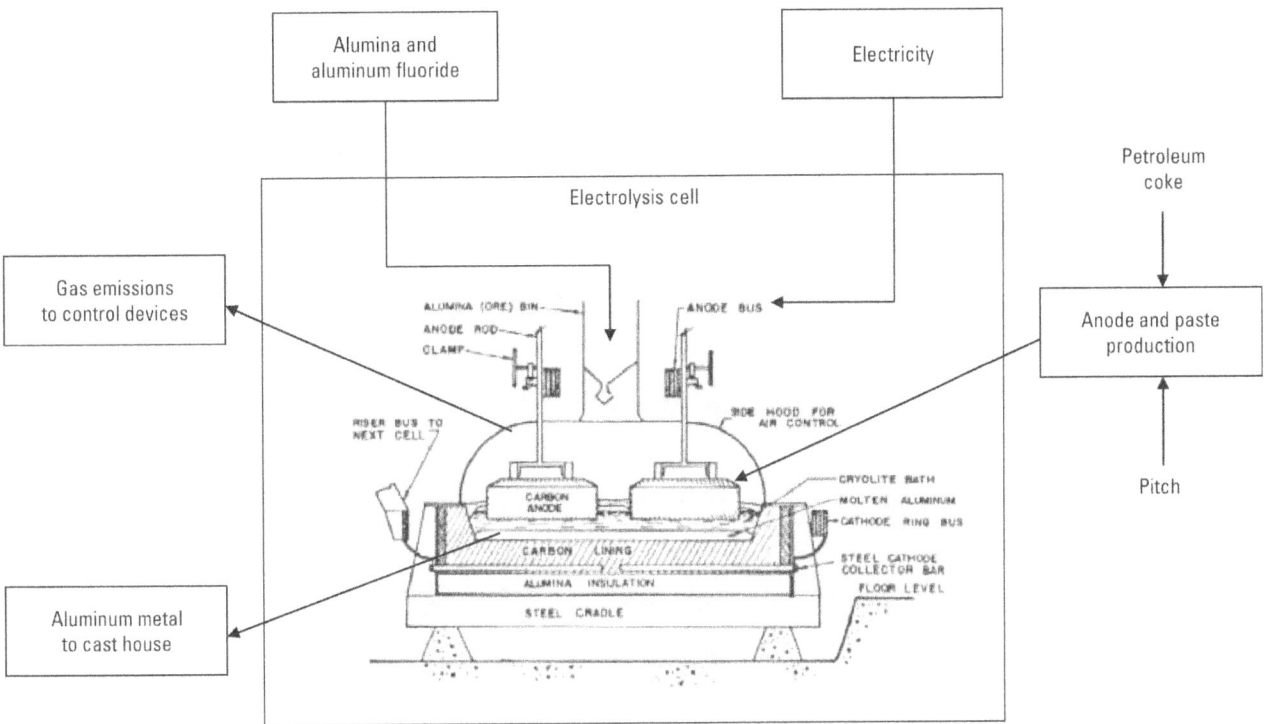

Figure 6. Diagram showing a typical process flow for aluminum smelting. Copied by permission from the Electrochemistry Encyclopedia (*http://electrochem.cwru.edu/encycl/*) on March 1, 2010; the original material is subject to periodic changes and updates.

Anodes are critical to aluminum reduction. They carry the electric charge (which drives the reaction) to the cryolite (the alumina solvent) in the reduction cell, and they provide the carbon (which causes the anode to be continuously consumed) for the reduction reaction that strips the oxygen from the alumina and removes it to the atmosphere as carbon dioxide. There are two primary technologies used to produce anodes for the Hall-Héroult process—Söderberg and prebake. Söderberg anodes begin as semiliquid constructions that are continuously fed into the molten cryolite bath. Prebaked anodes are preformed and hardened in gas-fired ovens at high temperatures. Prebaked anodes are then fed into the cryolite bath. The major difference is that the Söderberg anode hardens with heat generated from the electrolytic process as it descends into the cryolite bath, and the prebaked anode is hardened before use in the electrolytic cell. The newest and largest aluminum smelters generally use prebaked anodes, which are more efficient.

To produce a prebaked anode, petroleum coke and pitch are blended together and baked in ovens. Anode manufacturing generates additional materials flows. Figures 7 through 10 show selected materials flows for the anode-making process of model European and World plants in 2005 (European Aluminium Association, 2008). Figure 7 shows the inputs and outputs to produce 1 t of anode. European anode plants require 3 percent more thermal energy than World anode plants and 12 percent more electricity; however, the European plants produce slightly less air (fig. 8) and water emissions and significantly less solid wastes (fig. 9). European anode plants recycle slightly more refractory materials and slightly less steel than World plants but significantly more other solid wastes (fig. 10).

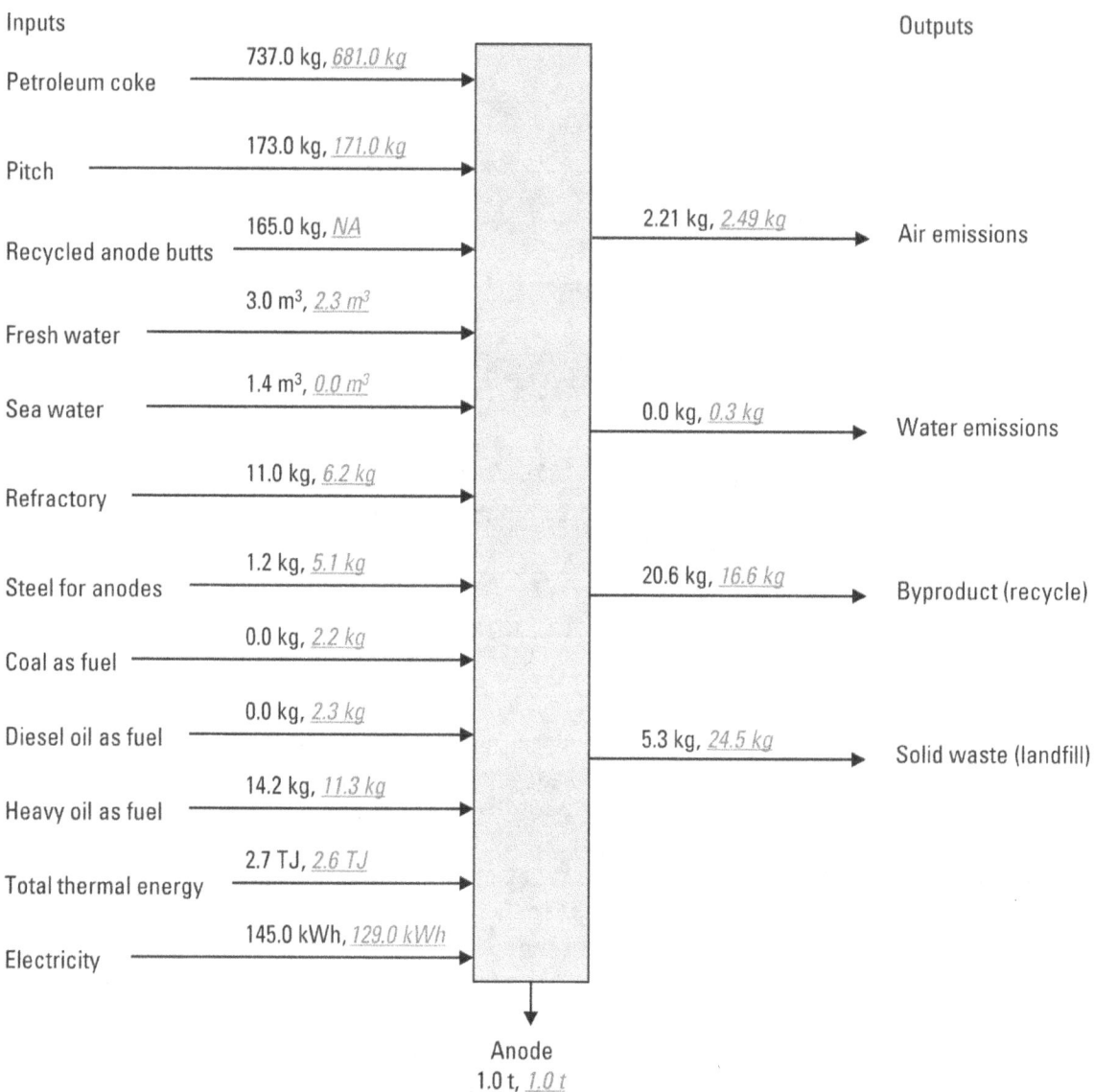

Figure 7. Diagram showing selected materials flows for the anode-making process of model European and World plants. European model data are in plain black text, and World model data are in underlined red italic text. Data are from European Aluminium Association (2008, p. 24). NA, not available; kg, kilogram; kWh, kilowatthour; m^3, cubic meter; t, metric ton; TJ, terajoule. Greenhouse gases are discussed separately in the text.

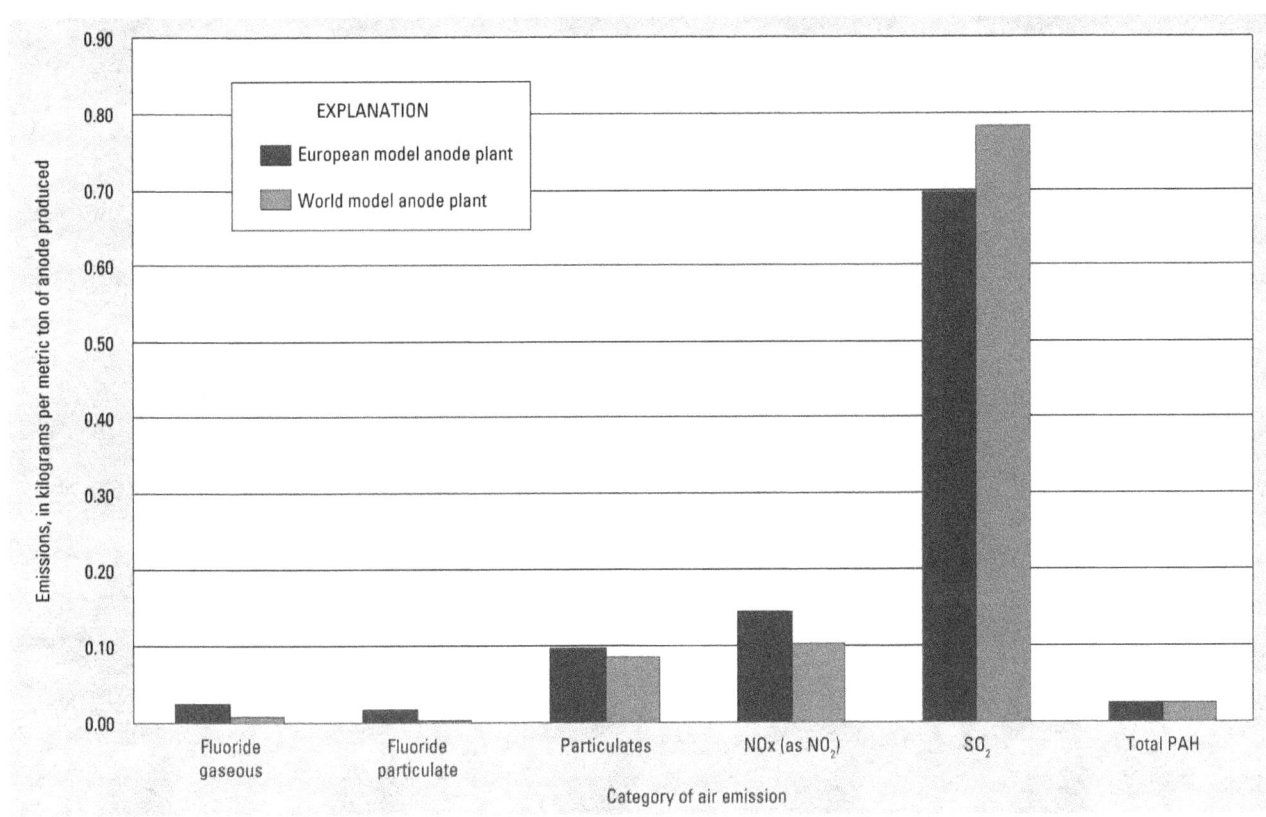

Figure 8. Bar chart showing air emissions for the anode-making process of model European and World plants. Gaseous fluoride and fluoride particles are expressed as contained fluorine. NOx, nitrous oxide; NO2, nitrogen dioxide; PAH, polycyclic hydrocarbon; SO2, sulfur dioxide.

23

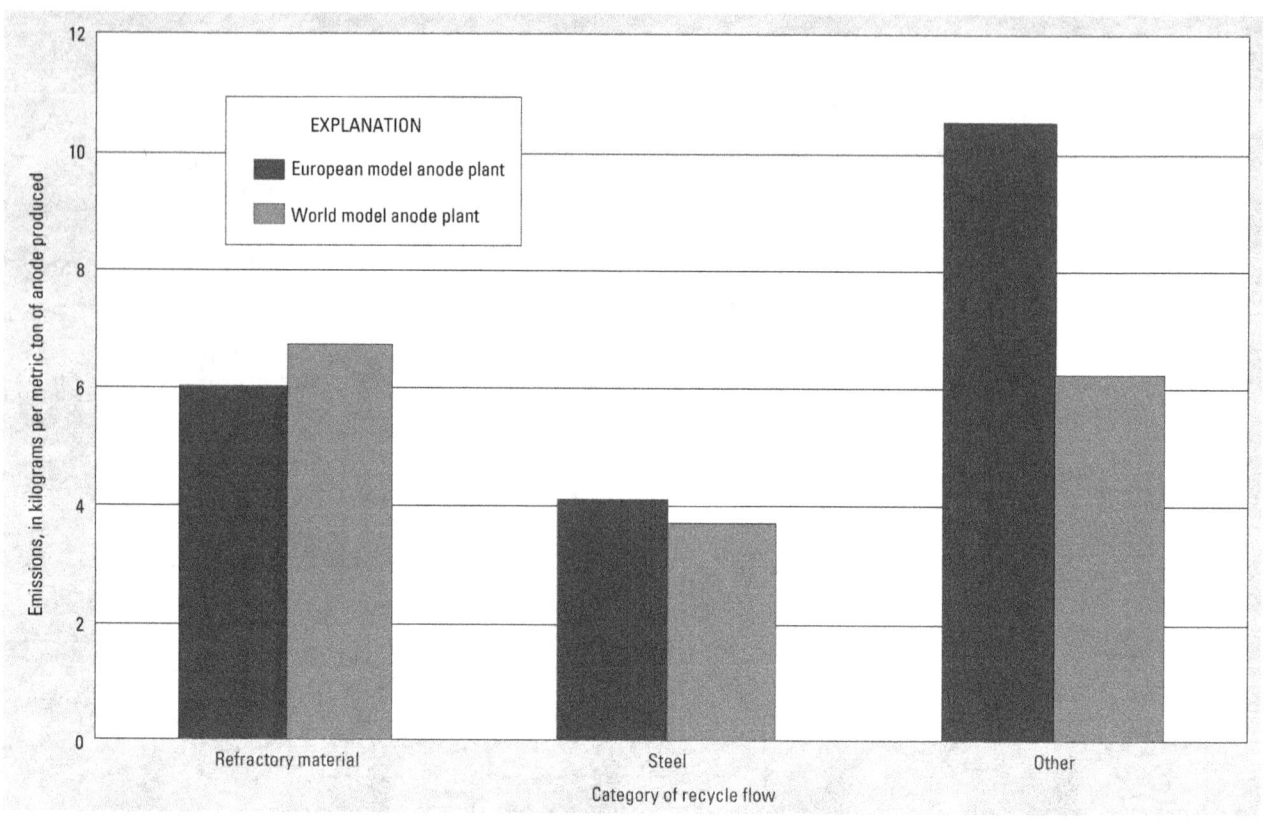

Figure 9. Bar chart showing externally recycled waste products for the anode-making process of model European and World plants.

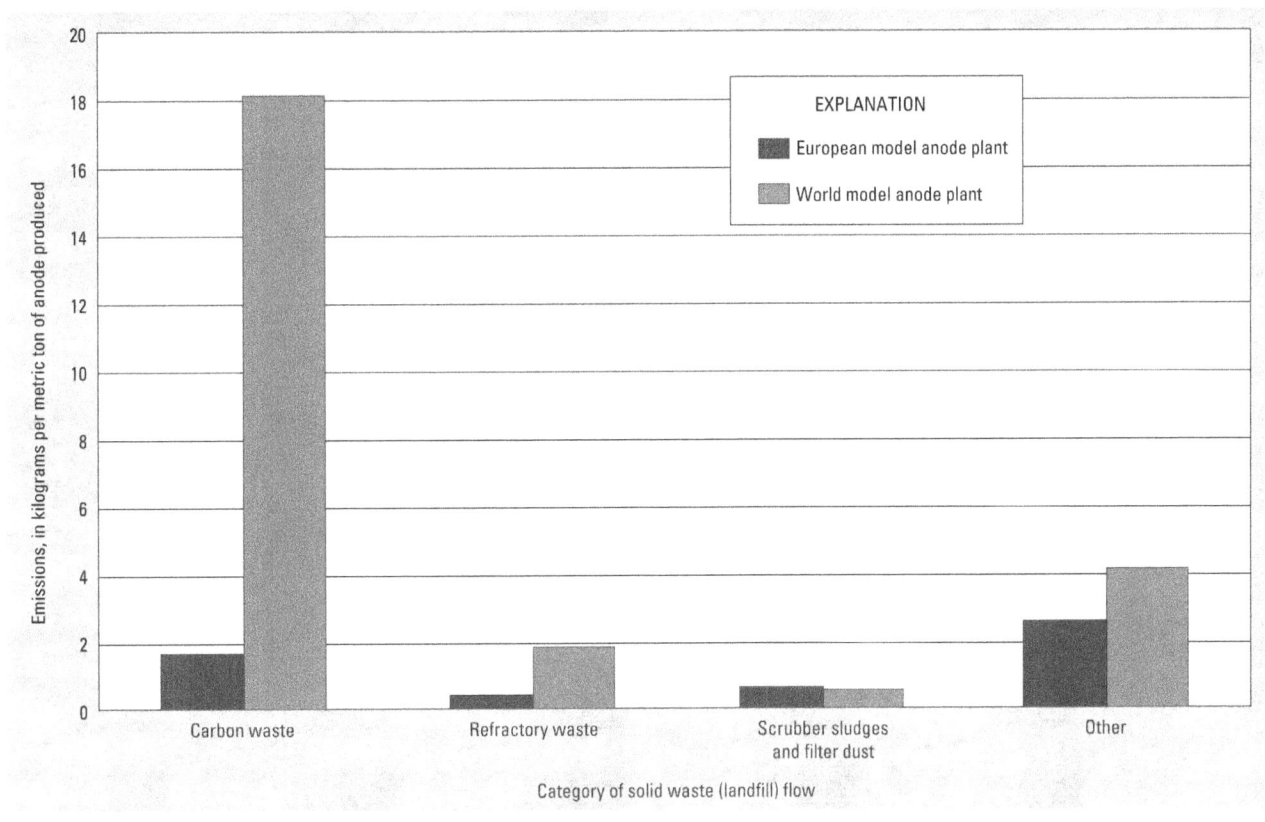

Figure 10. Bar chart showing solid waste (landfill) for the anode-making process of model European and World plants.

In the European and World models of the aluminum smelting process, the salient input flows to produce 1 t of anode are, respectively, 737 kg and 681 kg of petroleum coke, 173 kg and 171 kg of pitch, 2.7 terajoules (TJ) and 2.6 TJ of fuel energy, and about 145 kilowatthours (kWh) and 129 kWh of electricity (figs. 7 through 10). The corresponding output flows (exclusive of GHGs) of significance are, respectively, 1.5 kg and 2.0 kg of SO_2 and 5.3 kg and 24.5 kg of various materials to landfill storage. Of primary environmental concern is the generation of GHG (CO_2).

The principal inputs to the aluminum smelting process are alumina, aluminum fluoride (AlF_2), carbon (as anodes), and electricity. The principal outputs are aluminum metal, CO_2, and some solid wastes. In the European and World models of the aluminum smelting process (Hall-Héroult process), the salient input flows to produce 1 t of aluminum metal are, respectively, 1.93 t and 1.92 t of alumina, about 428 kg and 435 kg of anode paste, and about 14,914 kilowatthours (kWh) and 15,289 kWh of electricity (figs. 11 through 15). In 1930, about 25 megawatthours per metric ton of aluminum was required (Rosenqvist, 2004, p. 449). The corresponding output flows (exclusive of GHGs) of significance are, respectively, 8.2 kg and 14.9 kg of SO_2, about 1.1 kg and 3.4 kg of fluorine to air (0.6 kg and 0.3 kg to water), and 28.5 kg and 33.2 kg of various materials to landfill storage.

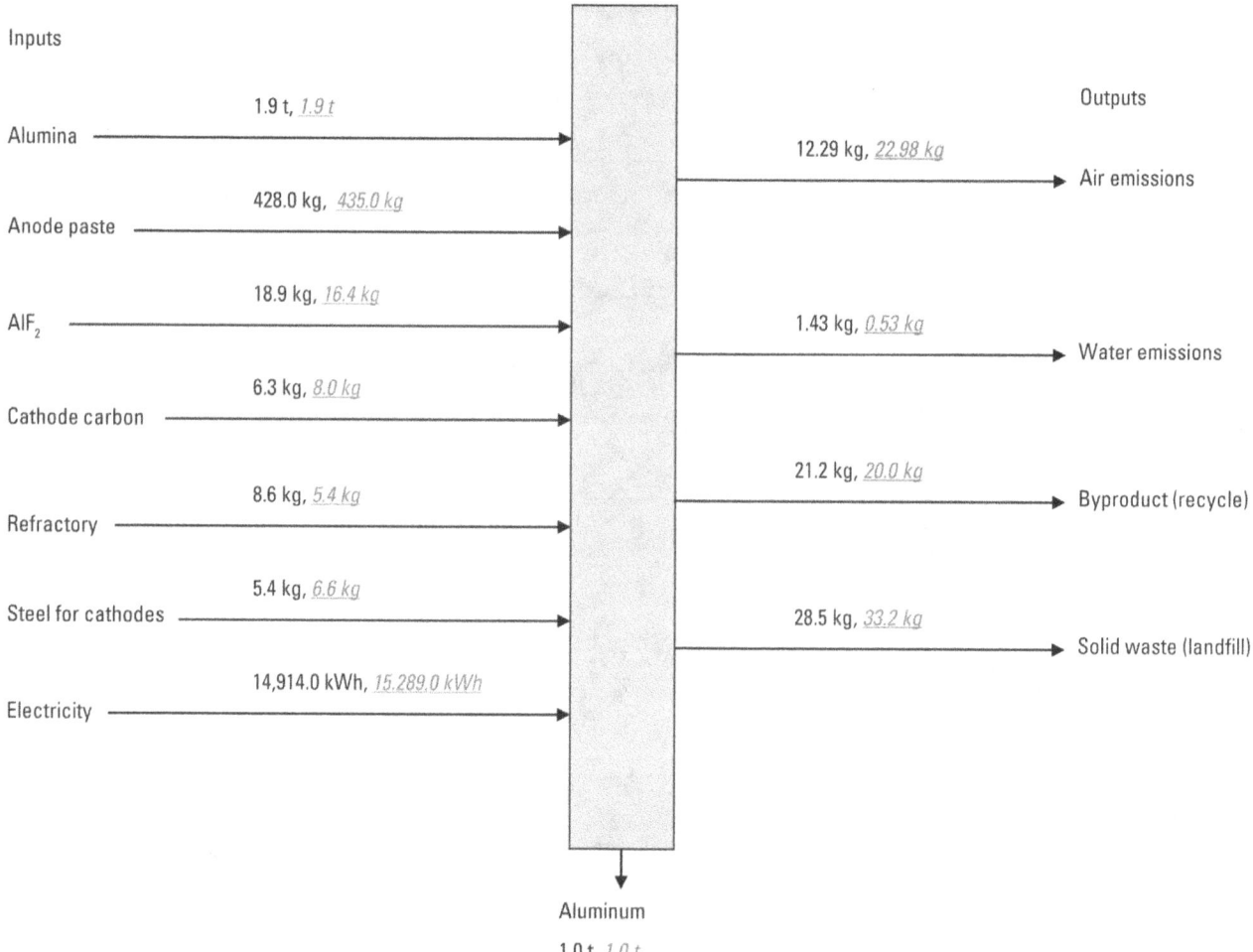

Figure 11. Diagram showing selected materials flows for models of European and World aluminum smelters. European model data are in plain black text, and World model data are in underlined red italic text. Data are from European Aluminium Association (2008, p. 27). kg, kilogram; kWh, kilowatthour; t, metric ton. Greenhouse gases are discussed separately in the text.

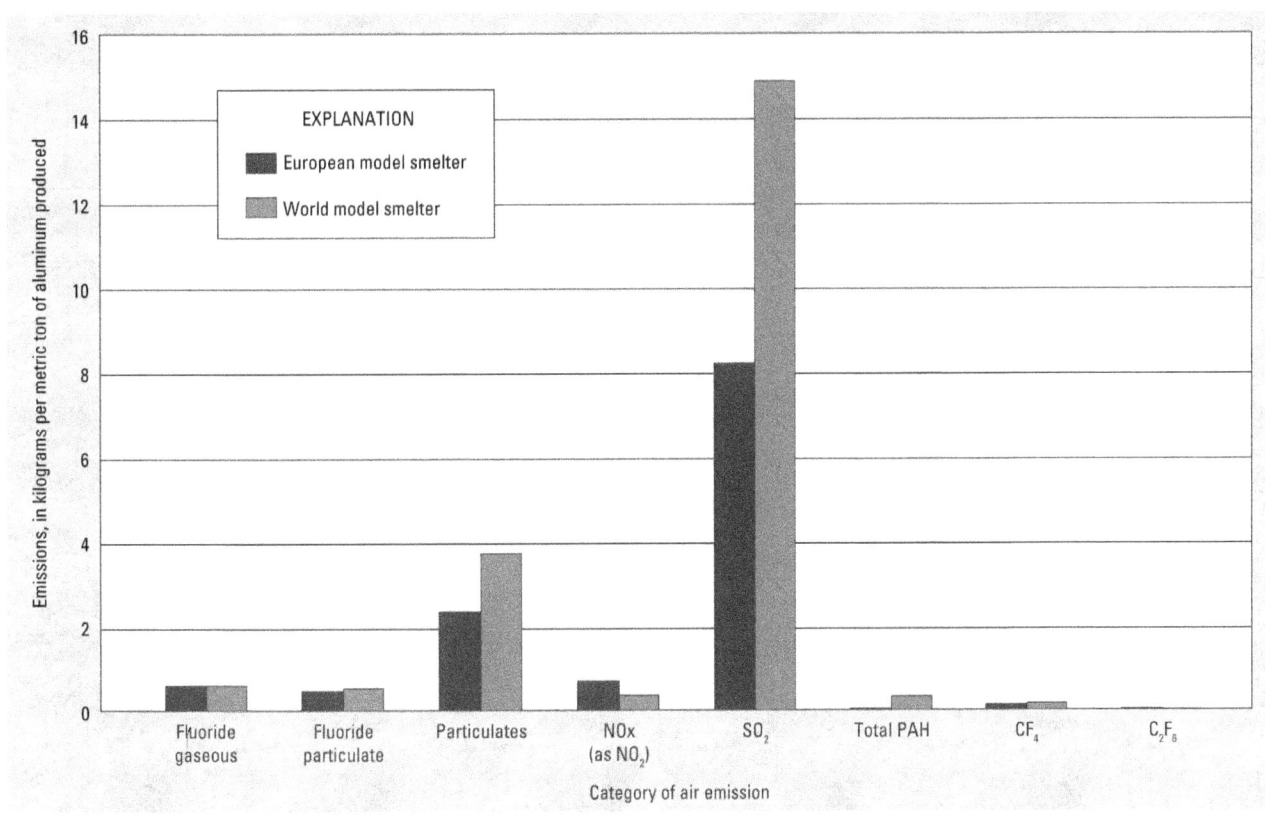

Figure 12. Bar chart showing air emissions for models of European and World aluminum smelters. NOx, nitrous oxide; NO_2, nitrogen dioxide; PAH, polycyclic hydrocarbon; SO_2, sulfur dioxide; CF_4, tetrafluoromethane; C_2F_6, hexafluoroethane.

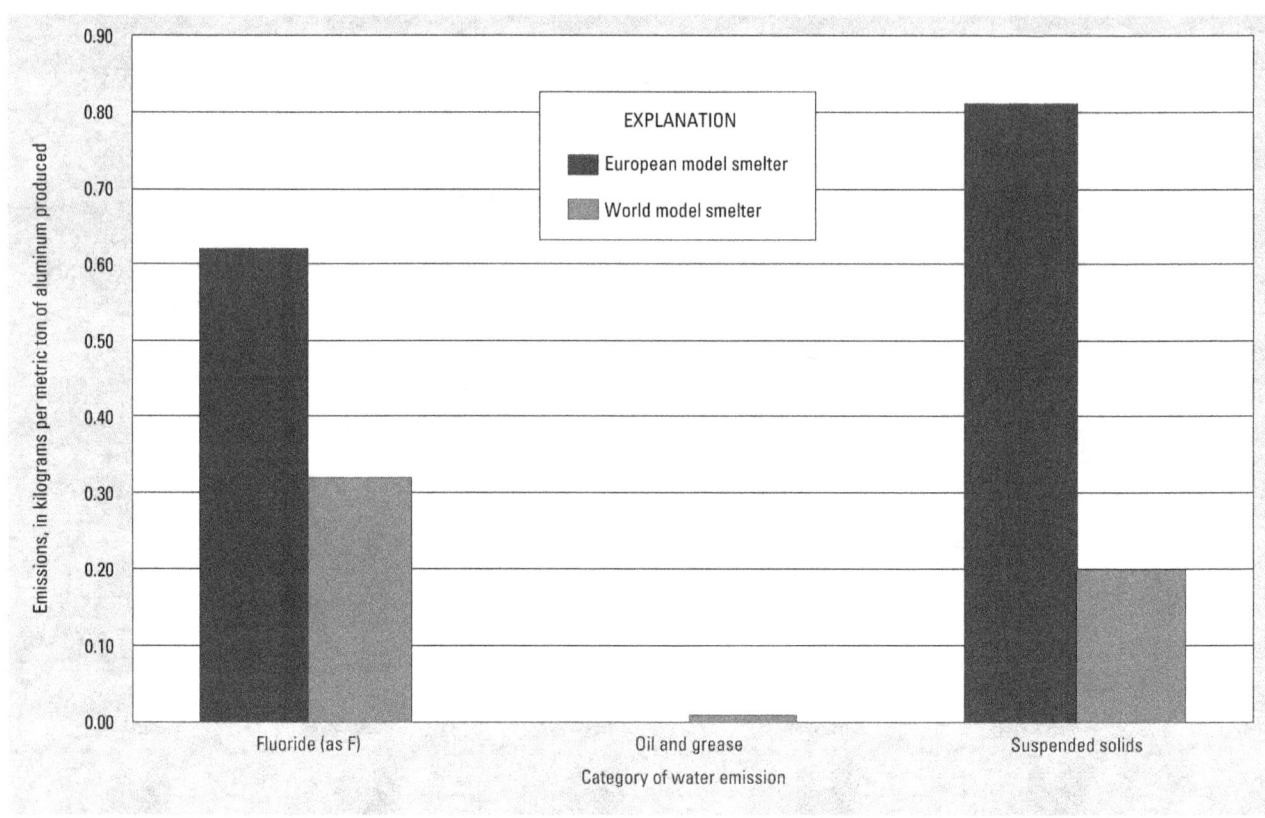

Figure 13. Bar chart showing emissions to water for models of European and World aluminum smelters. F, fluorine.

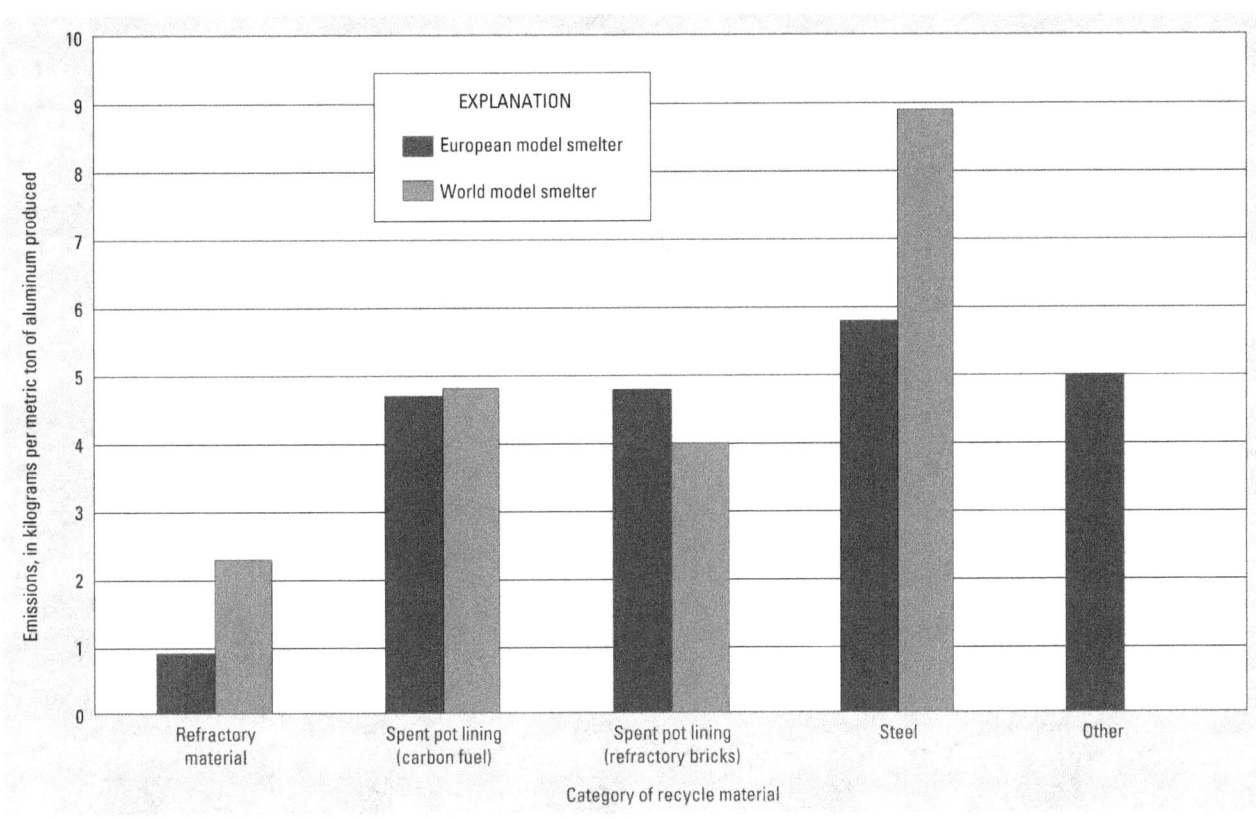

Figure 14. Bar chart showing externally recycled waste for models of European and World aluminum smelters.

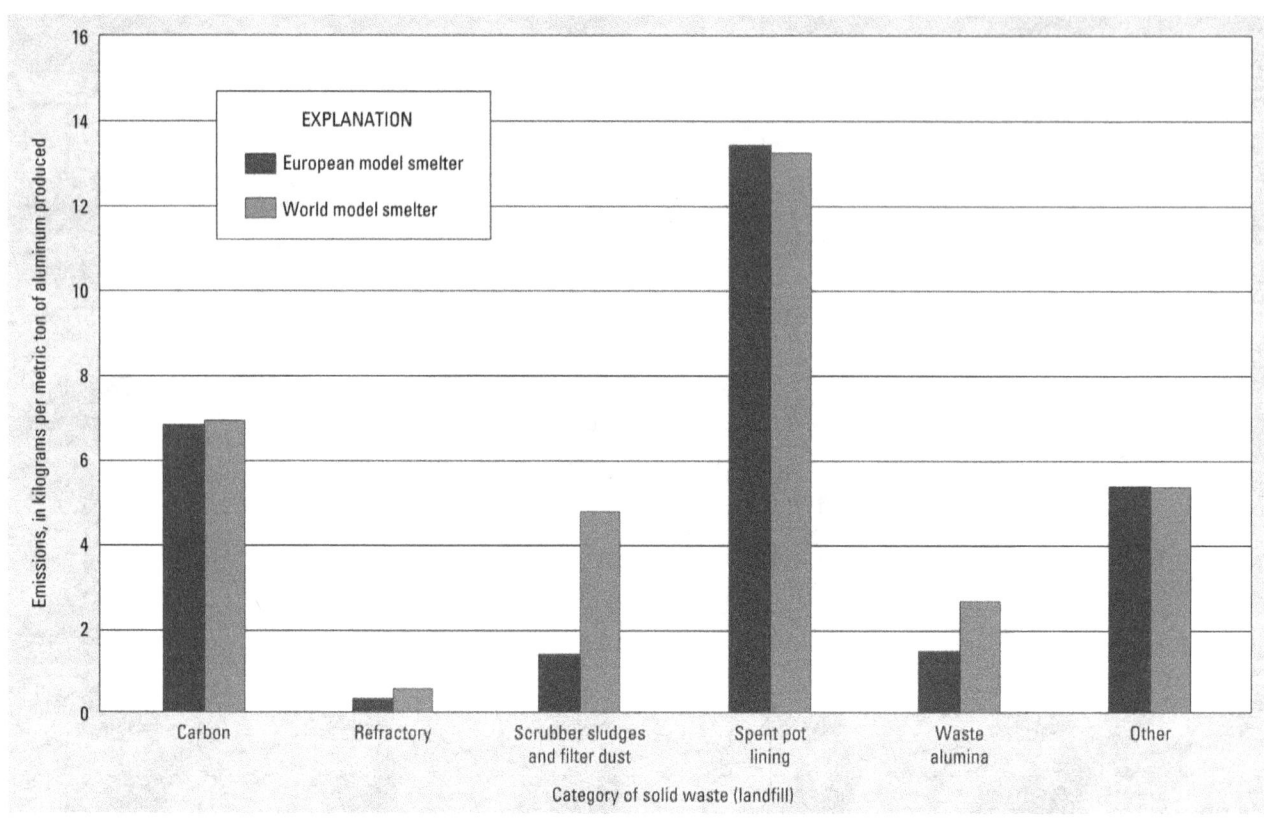

Figure 15. Bar chart showing solid waste for models of European and World aluminum smelters.

3.1.2.3.1. Aluminum Smelting and Electrolysis—Greenhouse Gas Emissions

A greenhouse gas (GHG) is an atmospheric gas that is believed to contribute to climate change by increasing the ability of the atmosphere to trap heat. Different species of such gases have differing abilities to trap heat. Global warming potential (GWP) is a measure of the relative effectiveness of a GHG to affect climate. The heat-trapping ability of 1 t of CO_2 is the common standard, and emissions are expressed in terms of CO_2 equivalent (CO_2e).

The burning of fossil fuels for energy production, transportation, and industrial activities is among the human activities that can contribute CO_2 and other GHG emissions to the atmosphere. Aluminum smelting is one of the industrial activities under study because the process emits significant quantities of carbon dioxide and some PFC gases.

Although PFCs emitted from aluminum smelters are not considered toxins or ozone-depleting gases (Simmonds and others, 2002), they are considered to be GHGs. PFCs are of particular concern because they have a greater GWP per unit of emission than CO_2. It has been estimated that 1 t of tetrafluoromethane (CF_4) has the equivalent GWP of 6,500 t of CO_2 and that 1 t of hexafluoroethane (C_2F_6) has the equivalent GWP of 9,200 t of CO_2 (U.S. Environmental Protection Agency, 2006; International Aluminium Institute, 2009c). Aluminum smelting and the manufacturing of electronic chips are the largest known anthropogenic sources of PFCs (Aslam and others, 2003; U.S. Environmental Protection Agency, 2006). Figure 16 shows the flows of fluorine within the aluminum smelting process. Available information is insufficient to calculate all the flow quantities; however, they are represented in the diagram as either a number reported for the World model smelter, or as "kg," indicating a flow of "unknown" kilograms of fluorine per metric ton of aluminum produced (European Aluminium Association, 2008).

PFCs have an extremely stable molecular structure relative to other anthropogenic gases in the atmosphere and are largely immune to the chemical processes that break down most atmospheric pollutants in the lower atmosphere. Not until the PFCs reach the mesosphere, about 60 kilometers above Earth, do very-high-energy ultraviolet rays from the Sun destroy them. This removal mechanism is extremely slow and, as a result, PFCs accumulate in the atmosphere and possibly remain there for several thousand years (U.S. Environmental Protection Agency, 2006).

In 2006, GHG emissions worldwide totaled about 51 billion metric tons (Gt). Taken together, the aluminum, copper, nickel, and steel industries accounted for 2.62 Gt, or about 5.2 percent of total GHG emissions. The USGS estimates, based on the relative production levels of aluminum, copper, nickel, and steel in 2008, that the aluminum industry contributed 0.45 Gt of CO_2e GHG.

Significant amounts of GHGs are emitted during the mining, concentrating, smelting, and refining of metals. Table 4 provides a perspective on how the process of producing aluminum from bauxite compares with processes for the production of other metals with regard to the generation of GHGs (Carbon Emitters, 2009).

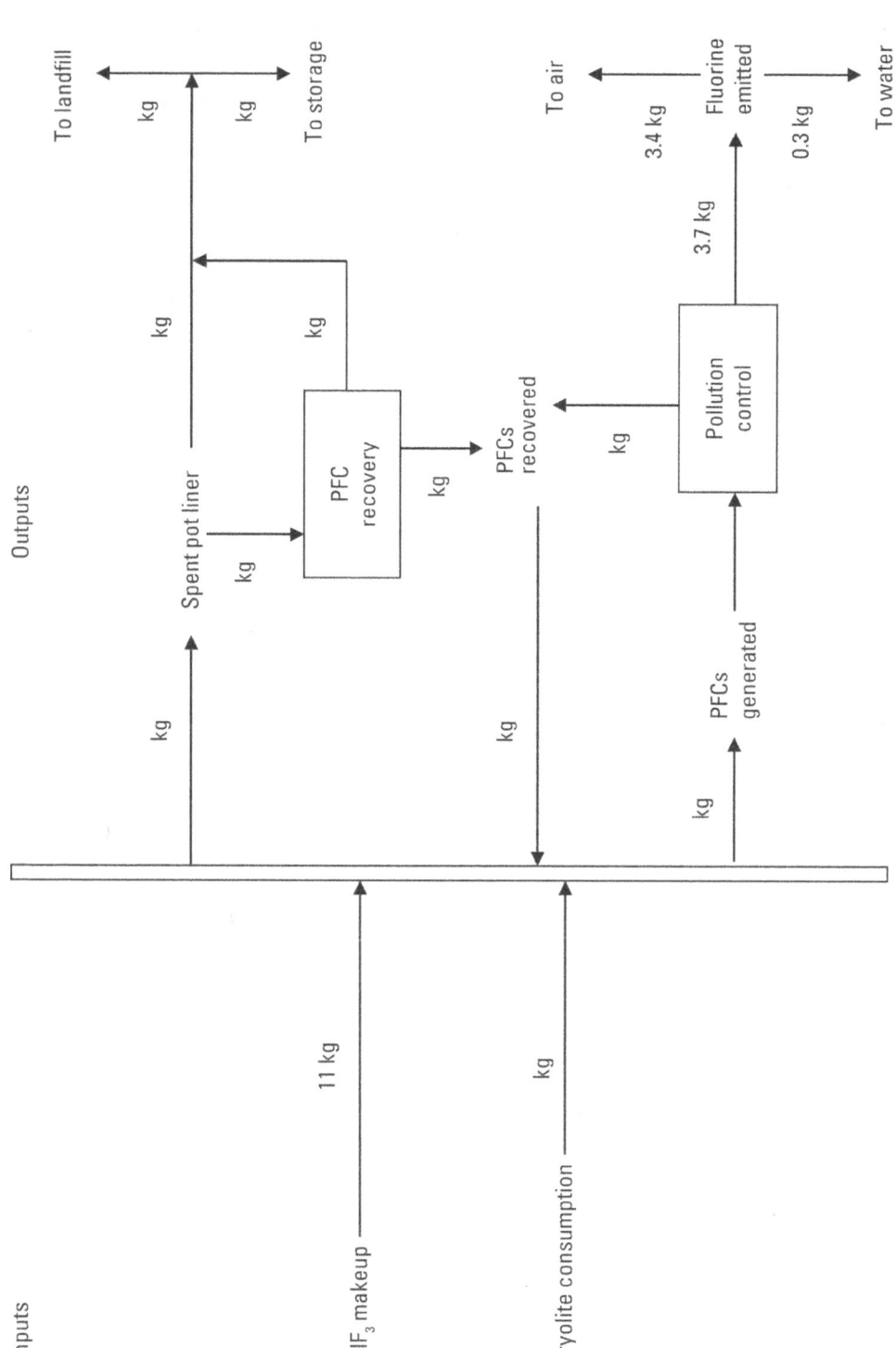

Figure 16. Diagram of sources and distribution of fluorine during aluminum smelting. Available information was insufficient to calculate all the flow quantities and a standalone "kg" is used to indicate a flow of "unknown" kilograms of fluorine per metric ton of aluminum produced. AlF₃, aluminum fluoride; kg, kilogram; PFC, perfluorocarbon.

Table 4. Selected metals industry contributions to greenhouse gas emissions in 2006.

[Data are from Carbon Emitters (2009). CO_2e, carbon dioxide equivalent]

Metal industry	Production, in million metric tons	Greenhouse gas emission, in billion metric tons of CO_2e	Share of world greenhouse gas emissions, in percent	Share of fossil fuel greenhouse gases, in percent
Aluminum	33	0.41	0.8	1.2
Copper	13.5	0.04	0.1	0.1
Nickel	1.4	0.04	0.1	0.1
Steel	1,250	2.13	4.2	6.3

Aluminum production generates not only PFCs during anode events (discussed separately below) but also large quantities of CO_2 from the use of electricity that is generated from the combustion of hydrocarbons, fuel, and process-generated reduction reactions. The World Business Council and the World Resource Institute have suggested a GHG reporting protocol that accounts for GHG generation on a corporate basis. GHGs attributable to imported materials and energy flows are accounted to the ex-corporate generator—for example, the GHG generated by hydrocarbon-originated electricity that is imported (across the corporate fence, for example, a public utility) would be considered as "indirect" with respect to the subject corporation (International Aluminium Institute, 2003).

Martchek (2007) calculated (based on a model of the global aluminum industry) the CO_2e emissions for the several steps of global aluminum production through semifabrication. Table 5 presents those results. Martchek estimated that the intensity of GHG emissions for the global aluminum industry (mining through semifabricated aluminum shipments) decreased to 8.2 t of CO_2e per metric ton of semifabricated aluminum shipped in 2005 from 11.0 t of CO_2e per metric ton of semifabricated aluminum shipped in 1990, and projected that the level will be 6.1 t of CO_2e per metric ton of semifabricated aluminum shipped in 2032. Drivers for the historic and expected improvement include increased recycling and lower emissions from primary aluminum smelters owing to technology improvements (Martchek, 2007).

Table 5. Greenhouse gas emission intensity of primary aluminum operations in 2005.

[Unless specified otherwise, units are in kilograms (kg) of carbon dioxide equivalent per metric ton of aluminum (CO_2e/t_Al). Perfluorocarbons (PFCs) are weighted higher than CO_2 for global warming potential (GWP); in terms of GWP, 1 metric ton (t) of carbon tetrafluoride (CF_4) is equivalent to 6,500 t of CO_2, and 1 t of hexafluoroethane (C_2F_6) is equivalent to 9,200 t of CO_2. NA, not available; XX, not applicable. Data are from Martchek (2007)]

Contributor	Production step				Mining through smelting	
	Mining	Refining	Anodes	Smelting	Quantity	Percentage of CO_2e/t_Al
Electricity	NA	58	63	5,147	5,268	57.0
Fuels	16	754	135	133	1,038	11.2
Perfluorocarbons	NA	NA	NA	960	960	10.4
Process	NA	NA	388	1,582	1,970	21.3
Total	16	812	586	7,822	9,236	XX
Percentage of total	0.17	8.79	6.34	84.69	XX	XX

3.1.2.3.2. Aluminum Smelting and Electrolysis—Generation of PFCs (Anode Events)

The normal reduction process is represented by the following chemical equation:

$$2Al_2O_3 + 3C \rightarrow 4Al + 3CO_2. \tag{1}$$

On occasion, there is an overvoltage disturbance in the cell. These episodes, termed "anode events," are triggered by an insufficient amount of alumina in the cell. The anode event causes the fluorine contained in the cryolite and aluminum fluoride to react with the carbon anodes to form the gases tetrafluoromethane (CF_4) and hexafluoroethane (C_2F_6), often referred to as perfluorocarbons (PFCs). An anode event is represented by the following chemical equation:

$$Na_3AlF_6 + nC \rightarrow (CF_2)n \rightarrow CF_4, C_2F_6. \tag{2}$$

A typical anode event may have a duration of approximately 2 minutes and have a frequency of 0.2 to 1.5 cells per day for a smelter with 150 to 300 cells (Fraser and others, 2009). The frequency and duration of anode events have been reduced considerably since the late 20th century as old plants are phased out and new plants are constructed with improved monitoring of the cell conditions in the molten "bath" and advances in plant design.

3.1.2.3.3. Industry Performance Goals

The IAI and its member companies have adopted through the Alumina for Future Generations program a number of performance targets related to the release of certain production wastes. Among these goals is the reduction of PFC emissions by 2020 to 50 percent of 2006 levels. This corresponds to a level of emissions of .5 t of CO_2e per metric ton of aluminum. The IAI has adopted a goal of achieving a 33 percent reduction from the 1990 level of 2.4 kg of fluorine per metric ton of aluminum produced by 2010. IAI also adopted a goal to reduce the amount of electrical energy used in aluminum smelting by 10 percent to 14.5 megawatthours (MWh) from 1990 levels by 2010. Finally, IAI adopted a goal of reducing energy use per metric ton of alumina refined by 10 percent from 2006 levels to 14.4 gigajoules per metric ton of aluminum by 2020 (International Aluminium Institute, 2009a).

3.1.2.4. Materials Inputs to and Outputs from Secondary Aluminum Production

Secondary aluminum is recovered from the processing of various kinds of aluminum scrap, including casting alloys, dross (a mixture of alumina, metal, and other materials), packaging, turnings, used beverage cans, wire and cable, and wrought alloys,. Alumina (Al_2O_3) that comes into the remelting system or that is generated within the system cannot be thermodynamically reduced to aluminum and therefore leaves the system as a nonmetallic residue, which ultimately is sold to the cement industry or used as backfill for mine recovery.

For primary aluminum production, there are environmental concerns about GHGs (CO_2, CF_4, and C_2F_6) and land use for mining and disposal of red mud (Bayer process residue) and smelter wastes (spent pot liner and other). Recovering aluminum from scrap to produce secondary aluminum ingot consumes about 6 percent of the energy required to produce primary aluminum. This significant energy difference is responsible for the emphasis placed on aluminum recycling in today's society and in the aluminum industry. Furthermore, to achieve a given output of ingot, recycled aluminum requires only about 10 percent of the capital equipment costs compared with those required for the production of primary aluminum (BCS, Inc., 2007, p. 64). Fluorocarbon gases are not produced with secondary smelting. The principal GHG is CO_2 and, because of the lower energy consumption, very much less is generated than is produced in primary smelting.

Boin and Bertram (2005) reported on the efforts of 15 European Union members to construct a model for secondary aluminum in Europe—European Scrap Smelting Unit Model (ESSUM). In 2002, ESSUM showed that producing 1 t of aluminum metal alloy required 936 kg of scrap, 81 kg of turnings, 33 kg of alloys, 33 kg of dross, 16 kg of oxide, and 2 kg of salt (fig. 17).

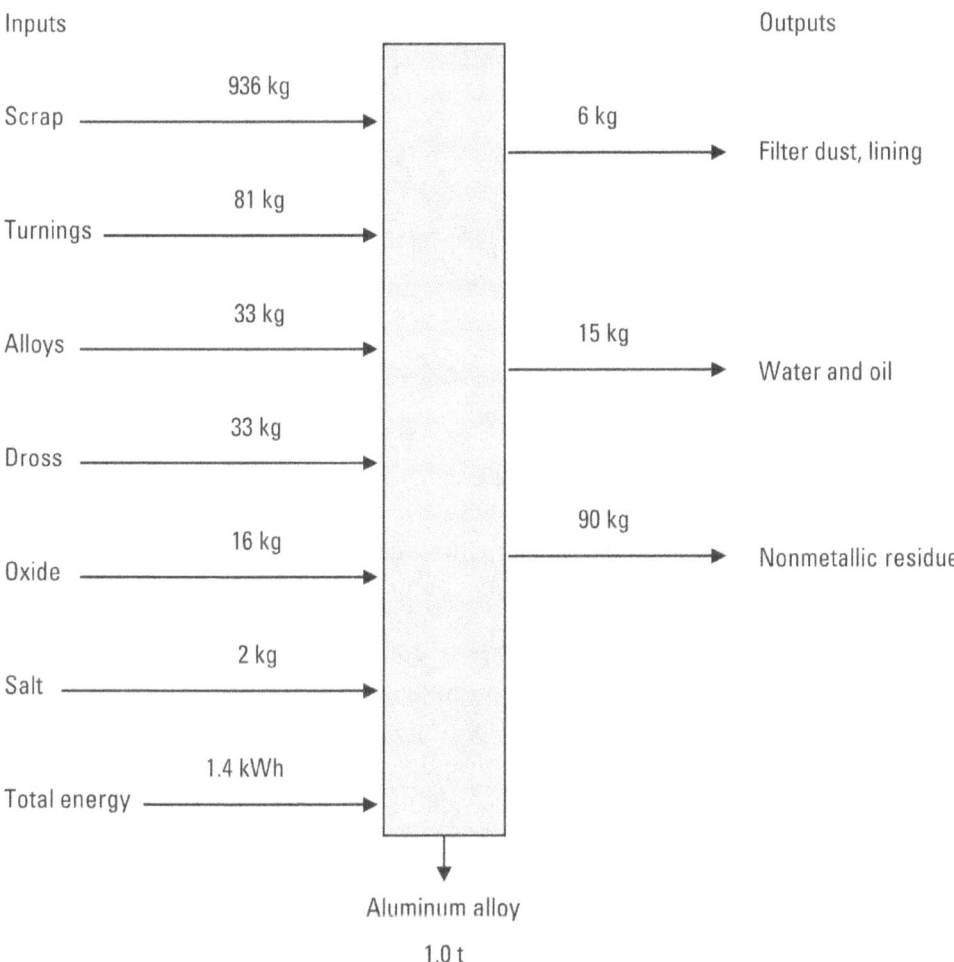

Figure 17. Diagram showing selected material flows for a European secondary aluminum smelter model in 2002. Data are from European Aluminum Association (2008). kg, kilogram; kWh, kilowatthour; t, metric ton.

Scrap for processing in secondary smelters can come from many sources and can be of various types. One convenient means to categorize scrap generation is by life cycle stage, which would include production (smelting), fabrication (making usable shapes of various alloys for further processing), manufacturing (machining shapes to make parts for assemblies), and end-of-life (recovery of old scrap from economic sectors). Scrap can also be assigned to different processing modes. Remelters usually operate flux-free furnaces that treat clean, identified, and essentially new scrap generated from fabrication and manufacturing operations. Remelters make specific alloys, usually for wrought products. Refiners deal with dross (skimmings) foundry scrap, and much of the end-of-life scrap. Refiners make foundry alloys and deoxidation alloys for the steel industry.

The difference in the generation of gas between primary and secondary aluminum smelting is significant. One investigator estimated GHG emissions (from the production of alumina through the casting of primary aluminum) within the EU27 to be about 11 Mt of CO_2e whereas secondary remelting and refining generated 0.88 Mt and 0.96 Mt of CO_2e, respectively. The substitution of secondary for primary aluminum product can significantly reduce GHG emissions (Fraunhofer Institute for Systems and Innovations Research, 2009).

Secondary aluminum processing is heavily dependent on natural gas consumption. Furnaces that use natural gas can generate NOx, which is a precursor to ozone (Metals Advisor, 2010). Life cycle analysis could be used to measure NOx and to develop strategies to reduce emissions.

3.1.3. Global Mass Flows of Aluminum—Consumption

3.1.3.1. Consumption—Overview

IAI has summarized the disposition of aluminum as a total in finished products (40.4 Mt in 2006) and as net additions to products in use (24.4 Mt in 2006), which are distributed among the following end uses:

- buildings (32 percent)
- engineering and cable (28 percent)
- packaging (1 percent)
- transportation (28 percent), including automobiles (16 percent)
- other (11 percent)

This section examines the apparent consumption of aluminum for the 20 most populous countries to show how aluminum consumption varies among countries. The next section will examine consumption by end use.

Consumption of aluminum can be measured at different points in the cycle of material use. Consumption can be measured either as the quantity of material that goes into goods manufactured within the country (industrial consumption) or as the quantity of material in goods consumed by inhabitants of the country (final consumption). Industrial consumption can be easily estimated as the amount of aluminum produced in the country plus imports of aluminum less exports of aluminum. Final consumption is much more difficult to measure as it requires at a minimum knowledge of the goods consumed and their aluminum content.

Previous studies (DeYoung and Menzie, 1999; Menzie, DeYoung, and Steblez, 2001) have shown that industrial consumption per capita in a country is related to the average national income level of the country as measured by GDP per capita. Table 6 presents data on and figure 18 is a plot of the aluminum consumption per capita versus the GDP per capita in 2006 for the 20 most populous countries (which are, in order of population, China, India, the United States, Indonesia, Brazil, Pakistan, Bangladesh, Russia, Nigeria, Japan, Mexico, Philippines, Vietnam, Germany, Ethiopia, Egypt, Turkey, Iran, Thailand, and France). Together these countries consumed 30.3 Mt of aluminum in 2006, or about two-thirds of global production. In general, countries with a GDP per capita of less than $5,000 consume less than 5 kg of aluminum per capita; countries with a GDP per capita between $5,000 and $15,000 consume between 5 and 10 kg of aluminum per capita; and countries with per capita incomes of greater than $25,000 consume between 15 and 35 kg of aluminum per capita. The change in per capita consumption that accompanies an increase in income is dramatic and is an important factor in understanding the likely future consumption of aluminum both at a country level and globally.

Table 6. Aluminum consumption per capita versus gross domestic product per capita for the 20 most populous countries in 2006.

[GDPpp, gross domestic product purchasing power parity; GDP/c pp, gross domestic product per capita purchasing power parity. GDPpp data are from the International Monetary Fund World Economic Outlook Data Base (October 2009); population data are from the U.S. Census Bureau International Data Base (March 2010); aluminum consumption data are from USGS Minerals Yearbook 2007, v. I and III]

Country	Population, in millions	GDPpp, in billion dollars	Aluminum consumption, in thousand metric tons	GDP/c pp, in dollars	Aluminum consumption per capita, in kilograms per capita
China	1,304	$8,220	8,648	$6,300	6.63
India	1,108	3,770	1,080	3,400	0.97
United States	298	12,500	9,173	42,000	30.74
Indonesia	232	858	288	3,700	1.24
Brazil	192	1,610	1,044	8,400	5.45
Pakistan	166	399	34	2,400	0.21
Bangladesh	150	315	24	2,100	0.16
Russia	142	1,520	1,047	10,700	7.37
Nigeria	140	140	11	1,000	0.08
Japan	128	3,910	3,393	30,700	26.61
Mexico	107	1,080	725	10,100	6.75
Philippines	95	486	26	5,100	0.28
Vietnam	85	256	88	3,000	1.03
Germany	82	2,460	2,619	29,800	31.78
Ethiopia	77	62	0	800	0.00
Egypt	74	326	110	4,400	1.48
Turkey	74	582	433	7,900	5.88
Iran	65	526	168	8,100	2.59
Thailand	65	537	407	8,300	6.29
France	63	1,900	945	30,000	14.92

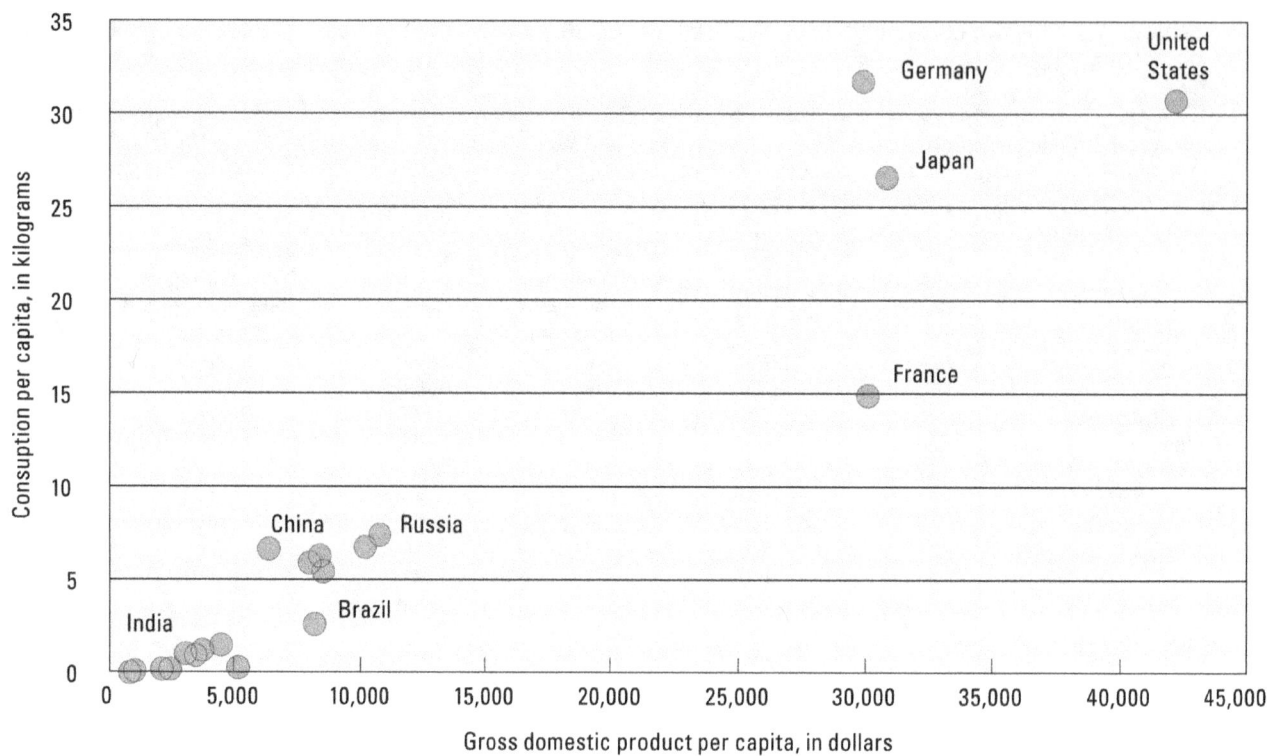

Figure 18. Graph showing aluminum consumption per capita measured against gross domestic product per capita for the 20 most populous countries in 2006.

3.1.3.2. Consumption—End Uses

This section presents statistics on the end uses of aluminum for selected populous countries, including Argentina, Brazil, China, France, Germany, India, Japan, Mexico, Russia, the United Kingdom, and the United States. Table 7 presents data on the percentage of aluminum consumption for various end uses in these countries. The data are available for different years and use somewhat different end-use classifications, which limit the conclusions that can be drawn from the data.

Table 7. Percentage of aluminum consumption by end use in populous countries with developing economies and selected high-income countries.

[XX, not applicable. Data are from Boltramovich, Dudarev, and Gorelov (2003, p. 126), Indian Bureau of Mines (2008), and Associação Brasileira do Alumínio (undated)]

End use	Developing economies					
	Argentina (2008)	Brazil (2008)	China (2009)	India (2007)	Mexico	Russia
Construction	21.4	11.3	40	13	6	7
Transportation	22	25.8	18	18	38	19
Electrical (power)	15.7	11.6	12	31	21	18
Durable goods	6.9	8.7	11	12	9	10
Packaging	19.3	28.7	9	11	6	3
Machinery and equipment	4.7	4	8	6	12	40
Fabricated metal	6.3	XX	XX	XX	XX	XX
Others	4.1	9.9	2	9	8	3

Table 7. Percentage of aluminum consumption by end use in populous countries with developing economies and selected high-income countries.—Continued

[XX, not applicable. Data are from Boltramovich, Dudarev, and Gorelov (2003, p. 126), Indian Bureau of Mines (2008), and Associação Brasileira do Alumínio (undated)]

| | High-income countries | | | | | |
	France (2004)	Germany (2006)	United Kingdom (2006)	Western Europe (2006)	Japan (2006)	United States (2006)
Construction	21	16.0	30	25	13.2	13.0
Transportation	36	44.1	21	36	40.5	38.0
Electrical	XX	6.0	XX	XX	4.5	5.0
Durables	XX	4.6	XX	XX	XX	7.0
Packaging	10	9.3	21	17	10.2	26.0
Machinery	XX	8.4	XX	XX	3.9	7.0
Engineering	31	XX	28	14	XX	XX
Fabricated metal	XX	5.6	XX	XX	11.6	XX
Other	2	6.0	XX	8	16.1	4.0

Nevertheless, the data when combined with data on the GDP per capita do suggest that several important changes in the consumption of aluminum occur as income increases. First, the data show that aluminum consumption for electrical end uses decreases with increasing income (fig. 19). Second, the data show that aluminum consumption for transportation end uses increases with rising income (fig. 20).

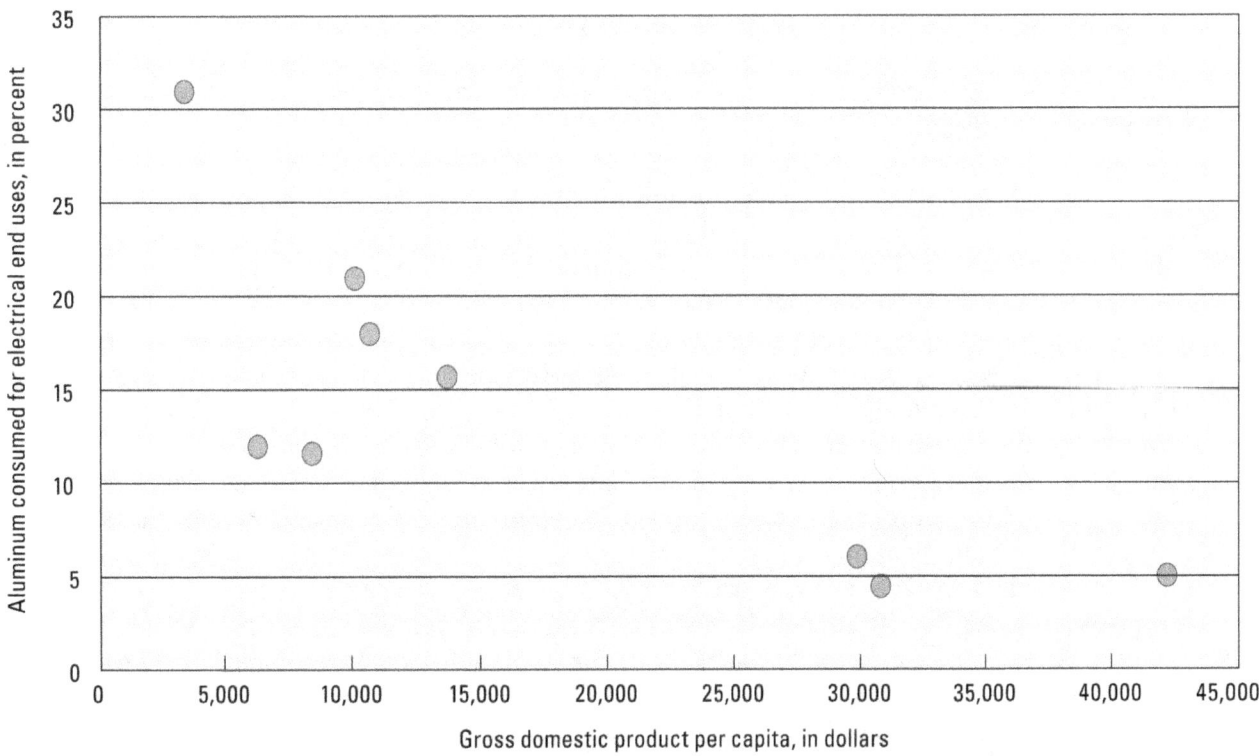

Figure 19. Graph showing percentage of aluminum consumption in electrical end uses against gross domestic product per capita.

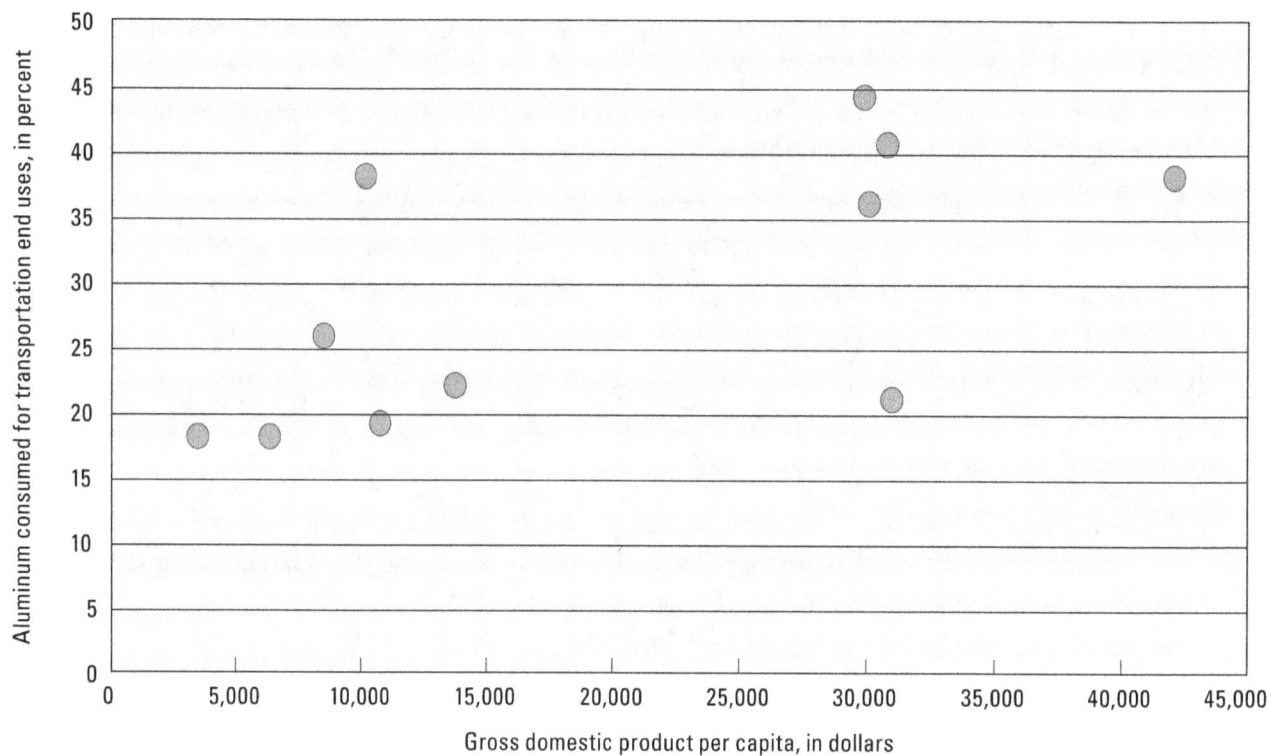

Figure 20. Graph showing percentage of aluminum consumption in transportation end uses against gross domestic product per capita.

These changes in the use of aluminum with income have important implications for aluminum recycling. Because aluminum in electrical systems is typically in service for long periods of time, the amount of aluminum available for recycling in countries with lower but rapidly growing incomes is likely to be delayed relative to countries with higher incomes. Transportation is the leading end use of aluminum in high-income countries, and automobiles are typically the leading use of aluminum in transportation. Because automobiles typically have in-service time periods of about 10 years, higher income countries have a larger supply of aluminum scrap available for trade or recycling than do countries that do not use automobiles for transportation or are only beginning to use automobiles as a primary mode of transportation. The transition from lower to higher incomes thus is accompanied by an increased availability of relatively easily recoverable aluminum. Of course, in-service times will create delays in the availability of this material.

Packaging is another end use that has a short in-service lifespan. Packaging, such as used beverage cans, can be easily collected, crushed, packaged, and recycled, and where widely used, they represent a ready source of post-consumer aluminum scrap. Use of aluminum packaging varies considerably, but inconsistently, with income. Factors other than income appear to play an important role in determining the proportion of aluminum used in packaging.

Because transportation becomes a more important component of aluminum end use as incomes rise, this study examines several components of the transportation end use in some detail.

3.1.3.2.1. Consumption for Transportation—Light Vehicles

The production and use of automobiles and light commercial vehicles is a major component of transportation and one that grows rapidly with rising income. Estimates of the amount of aluminum in

40

light vehicles can be calculated using statistics on vehicle production published by the International Organization of Motor Vehicle Manufacturers (OICA) (2007) and data on the intensity of use of aluminum in vehicles (Ducker Worldwide, LLC, 2008, p. 38). Ducker Worldwide, LLC (2008, p. 10) has published data on the aluminum content of vehicles by region or country for 2009 for North America, the European Union, Japan, a world average, the Republic of Korea, China, India and other Asia, Russia and other Europe, South America, and the Middle East. The company has published data for both 2006 and 2009 for North America, the European Union, and Japan (Ducker Worldwide, LLC, 2008, p. 10).

These data suggest that in 2006, aluminum use per vehicle was about 4 percent lower than in 2009. Therefore, the 2009 regional aluminum intensities were adjusted. Table 8 includes these adjusted (calculated) aluminum intensity data, along with vehicle production data, the estimated amount of aluminum used in light vehicles, aluminum consumption in 2006, and estimated aluminum consumption in transportation end uses. The calculated aluminum content of vehicles is the product of the number of vehicles and the estimate of the aluminum intensity of vehicles. The estimated consumption of aluminum is from the World Bureau of Metal Statistics. The estimated aluminum consumption in transportation end uses is based on World Bureau of Metal Statistics data and the transportation end-use percentages. About 69 million light vehicles were manufactured in 2006 containing approximately 7.8 Mt of aluminum for an average content of 113 kilograms per vehicle. Vehicles manufactured in North America contained the most aluminum, averaging 143 kilograms per vehicle, and vehicles manufactured in Africa and the Middle East contained the least aluminum, averaging 66 kilograms per vehicle.

Table 8. Vehicle production, aluminum intensity, aluminum use in light vehicles, aluminum consumption, and selected data on aluminum consumption in transportation end uses.

[XX, not applicable. Production data are from International Organization of Motor Vehicle Manufacturers (2007). Estimated data are rounded to no more than three significant digits]

Country	Total vehicles produced	Aluminum intensity, in kilograms per vehicle	Aluminum used in light vehicles, in metric tons	Aluminum consumption in 2006, in metric tons	Estimated aluminum consumption in transportation end uses, in metric tons
Argentina	432,101	67	28,951	145,600	32,000
Australia	330,900	78	25,810	439,600	XX
Austria	274,932	118	32,442	419,700	XX
Belgium	918,056	118	108,331	466,900	XX
Brazil	2,611,034	67	174,939	1,044,400	269,000
Canada	2,572,292	143	367,838	1,030,800	XX
China	7,188,708	96	690,116	8,648,100	1,560,000
Czech Republic	854,907	118	100,879	129,600	XX
Egypt	91,518	66	6,040	109,500	XX
Finland	32,770	76	2,491	72,500	XX
France	3,169,219	118	373,968	944,700	340,000
Germany	5,819,614	118	686,714	2,619,000	1,150,000
Hungary	190,823	118	22,517	224,800	XX
India	2,019,808	78	157,545	1,079,500	194,000
Indonesia	297,062	78	23,171	288,000	XX
Iran	904,500	66	59,697	168,400	XX
Italy	1,211,594	118	142,968	1,686,100	XX
Japan	11,484,233	110	1,263,266	3,392,600	1,370,000
Malaysia	502,973	78	39,232	193,400	XX
Mexico	2,045,518	143	292,509	724,700	275,000
Netherlands	159,454	118	18,816	146,400	XX
Poland	714,600	118	84,323	227,000	XX
Portugal	227,325	118	26,824	111,500	XX
Republic of Korea	3,840,102	104	399,371	1,153,200	XX
Romania	213,597	118	25,204	246,500	XX
Russia	1,508,358	76	114,635	1,047,000	199,000
Serbia	11,182	76	850	109,500	XX
Slovakia	295,391	118	34,856	25,500	XX
Slovenia	150,320	118	17,738	112,200	XX
South Africa	587,719	66	38,789	264,000	XX
Spain	2,777,435	118	327,737	862,800	XX
Sweden	333,168	118	39,314	138,400	XX
Taiwan	303,221	78	23,651	561,700	XX
Thailand	1,194,426	78	93,165	407,000	XX
Turkey	987,780	66	65,193	433,000	XX
Ukraine	295,260	76	22,440	39,500	XX
United Kingdom	1,648,388	118	194,510	566,500	119,000
United States	11,263,986	143	1,610,750	9,173,000	3,490,000
Uzbekistan	110,000	78	8,580	XX	XX
Others	531,606	108	57,413	XX	XX
Total	69,222,975	XX	7,803,584	XX	XX

The data on the aluminum content of vehicles give an estimate of the amount of material from this source that was added to total aluminum in use in 2006. When compared with the IAI global flow for 2006, these data indicate that light vehicles accounted for almost 20 percent of the aluminum in finished products and the percentage of aluminum in total products in automotive uses was 16 percent (Martchek, 2007). An estimate of the amount of aluminum that was used to manufacture the vehicles can be made by comparing shipments of aluminum to vehicle manufacturers in North America to the amount of aluminum contained in light vehicles manufactured in North America (table 9). These data indicate that, for every metric ton of aluminum in the vehicle, 1.046 t of aluminum was used to make the vehicle.

When the estimated aluminum content in light vehicles is compared with aluminum consumption and with estimates of aluminum consumption in the transportation end use (table 8), some inconsistencies are apparent. For example, the calculated aluminum content of vehicles for Slovakia exceeds the estimated aluminum consumption of the country in 2006. Also, the calculated aluminum content of vehicles exceeds the estimated aluminum content of transportation end uses for France and Mexico by about 6.5 percent and for the United Kingdom by 64 percent (table 10). Because Mexico is not a major manufacturer of aircraft, ships, or rail transportation, the difference may not indicate a major estimation problem. The large differences for France and the United Kingdom, however, are more serious. France manufactures aircraft in addition to vehicles, which would add to the size of the difference between aluminum reported in the end-use statistics versus aluminum calculated by estimating aluminum use by different modes of transportation. The estimated percentage of aluminum in transportation end uses for France is not unusual compared with the other high-income countries. The United Kingdom manufactures aircraft and builds ships in addition to light vehicles. The estimated percentage of aluminum consumption in transportation end uses for the United Kingdom (21 percent) is the lowest for high-income countries by a significant amount. When compared with the amount of aluminum calculated for light vehicles and not estimated for other modes of transportation, the low estimate for the transportation end use in the United Kingdom appears to be in error.

Table 9. Comparison of shipments of aluminum to manufacturers of passenger cars and light trucks with the estimated amount of aluminum contained in automobiles and light commercial vehicles in North America.

Aluminum shipments for passenger vehicles and light trucks in North America, in metric tons	2,375,000
Aluminum contained in automobiles and light commercial vehicles manufactured in North America, in metric tons:	
Canada	367,838
Mexico	292,509
United States	1,610,750
Total	2,271,100
Estimated scrap generated in manufacture, in metric tons	103,900
Percentage of shipments to scrap	4.4
Factor to estimate scrap from aluminum in vehicles	0.046

Comparison of aluminum used in the manufacture of vehicles with aluminum in transportation end uses in countries where vehicles are the main mode of transportation manufactured are in closer agreement (table 10). For example, transportation end-use data (about 32,000 t) for Argentina, which manufactures vehicles but not aircraft or ships, agree closely with the amount of aluminum that would be used in the manufacture of vehicles (about 30,000 t). Light vehicles account for 85 percent of the aluminum in transportation end uses in India, which has a small shipbuilding sector. Because the other countries with estimated aluminum consumption for transportation end uses have more complex transportation manufacturing sectors, analysis of the aluminum used in the manufacture of other modes of transportation will be necessary to further test the validity of the end-use data.

43

Table 10. Estimated amount of aluminum used to manufacture forms of transportation other than passenger cars and light trucks for selected countries.

[The calculated amount of aluminum shown for transportation end uses other than light vehicles is negative for France, Mexico, and the United Kingdom because the calculated aluminum content of light vehicles exceeds the estimated aluminum content for all transportation end uses. These differences likely indicate a measurement error or an error in a reported number. Data are rounded to no more than three significant digits]

Country	Estimated aluminum shipments for vehicles, in metric tons	Estimated aluminum for other forms of transportation, in metric tons	Estimated aluminum in transportation, in metric tons
Argentina	30,300	1,700	32,000
Brazil	183,000	86,000	269,000
China	722,000	838,000	1,560,000
France	391,000	-51,000	340,000
Germany	718,000	437,000	1,150,000
India	165,000	29,000	194,000
Japan	1,320,000	54,000	1,370,000
Mexico	306,000	-31,000	275,000
Russia	120,000	79,000	199,000
United Kingdom	203,000	-84,000	119,000
United States	1,680,000	1,810,000	3,490,000

The limited end-use data available and the inconsistencies in data classes point to a need for consistent end-use classes, for data for additional countries, and for more accurate data on aluminum end uses. Historical data for countries that have recently experienced rapid economic growth and transformation could improve estimates of future aluminum flows.

3.1.3.2.2. Consumption for Transportation—Aircraft

A second use of aluminum is in aircraft. IAI (2010) estimated that 80 percent of an aircraft's weight is aluminum. Table 11 presents estimates of the aluminum content of aircraft delivered in 2006 by Airbus, Boeing, Bombardier, and Embraer, respectively. Airbus has manufacturing and assembly facilities in France, Germany, Spain and the United Kingdom. Thus, it is difficult to assign the almost 19,000 t of aluminum in the aircraft delivered in 2006 to individual countries for comparison with country-level consumption data.

Table 11. Estimated aluminum content of Airbus, Boeing, Bombardier, and Embraer aircraft delivered in 2006.

[XX, not applicable. Data are from Airbus S.A.S. (2007); Aviation Today (2007); Empresa Brasileira de Aeronautica S.A. (2007); Airliners net (2010); The Boeing Company (2010). Totals may not add owing to independent rounding]

Aircraft model	Number delivered	Weight of one aircraft, in kilograms	Aluminum content, in metric tons
Airbus			
Single aisle	339	42,000	11,400
Wide body	86	99,000	6,810
Freighters	9	93,000	670
Total	434	XX	18,900
Average aluminum content per aircraft			43
Boeing			
717-200	5	31,892	128
737-600	10	37,104	297
737-700BBJ	10	42,895	343
737-700	108	38,147	3,300
737-800BBJ2	2	45,730	73
737-800	172	41,145	5,670
747-400	14	180,985	2,030
767-200	2	74,752	120
767-300	10	80,467	644
777-200	25	139,025	2,780
777-300	40	160,120	5,120
Total	398	XX	20,500
Average aluminum content per aircraft			51
Bombardier			
Regional airline aircraft:			
CRJ700/CRJ900	63	19,595	988
CRJ100/200 and CL601/604	49	11,500	451
Total	112	XX	1,440
Business aircraft:			
Challenger 300	55	10,140	446
Global jets	63	22,135	1,120
Lear 55/60	94	6,282	472
Total	212	XX	2,030
Average aluminum content per aircraft			11
Embraer			
Commercial aviation:			
ERJ 145	12	11,800	113
EMBRAER 170	35	20,150	564
EMBRAER 175	12	20,150	193
EMBRAER 190	40	27,100	867
EMBRAER 195	3	27,100	65
Total	98	XX	1,800
Executive aviation:			
Legacy 600	26	16,000	333
Legacy shuttle	1	16,000	13
Total	27	XX	346
Defense and government:			
EMBRAER 170	4	20,150	64
EMBRAER 190	1	27,100	22
Total	5	XX	86
Average aluminum content per aircraft			17

Boeing's principal manufacturing and assembly facilities are located in the United States. The majority of Bombardier's facilities are located in Canada, but some are in the United States. The principal manufacturing facilities of Embraer are located in Brazil. Boeing delivered aircraft containing about 20,500 t of aluminum. Bombardier's aircraft contained almost 3,500 t of aluminum; the proportion of aircraft built in the United States is unstated. Embraer delivered aircraft containing 2,200 t of aluminum in 2006.

It is not clear how much aluminum was used to build the aircraft as no data on shipments to aircraft manufacturers were available for the study. Data from Boeing (undated), however, indicate that the company offered 18,700 t of aluminum scrap for sale in 2006. If the Boeing's ratio of scrap plus aluminum in product to aluminum in product (approximately 2) is typical of other aircraft manufacturers, it suggests that 2 t of aluminum must be purchased for every ton of aluminum in the final product. Thus, vehicles and aircraft account for only 1.8 Mt of the 3.5 Mt of aluminum used for transportation end uses in the United States. In Brazil, about 4,400 t of aluminum was used to manufacture aircraft. Together, vehicles and aircraft account for 187,000 t of the 269,000 t of aluminum used in transportation end uses in Brazil.

3.1.3.2.3. Consumption for Transportation—Railcars

Based on data from FreightCar America, Inc. (2007), we estimate that about 410,000 t of aluminum was contained in railcars manufactured in the United States in 2006. Again, the amount of aluminum required to manufacture the rail cars is unknown, but if the ratio is similar to that calculated for aircraft, the amount of aluminum accounted for by light vehicles, civilian aircraft, and railcars in the United States would be about 2.5 Mt of the 3.5 Mt calculated from the transportation end use.

3.1.3.2.4. Consumption for Transportation—Final Thoughts

The data on the aluminum content of manufactured products seems to be reasonably accurate. For some of the products considered above, however, part of the aluminum could be aluminum alloy containing up to 10 percent alloying metals, such as copper and zinc. The amount of alloy used is unknown, and therefore no adjustment has been made to the calculated aluminum contents of products. If the aluminum contents are accurate, scrap ratios calculated for vehicles and aircraft could be conservative. Shipment data would be useful in resolving these issues.

Finally, data on the in-service times for the transportation systems would be useful for estimating the volumes of post-consumer scrap that are likely generated. Vehicles appear to have in-service times of 10 to 15 years. Based upon data from Jet Information Services (undated), aircraft appear to have in-service times of about 25 years. Jet Information Services (undated) also contains information on the number of aircraft removed from active inventory from 1965 to 2000 for aircraft manufactured by Western firms. In 2000, about 225 aircraft were removed from active inventory. Not all aircraft removed from active inventory are scrapped, but it appears that most are. If 75 percent of the aircraft were scrapped, then aluminum from about 170 aircraft was added to post-consumer scrap. Using the per aircraft aluminum content for Airbus and Boeing, which are the two largest Western aircraft manufacturers, this would generate between 7,300 and 8,700 t of post-consumer aluminum scrap.

3.2. Future Global Mass Flows of Aluminum

This section of the report examines future mass flows of aluminum for the short to medium term (to 2015) and for the longer term (2015 to 2025).

3.2.1. Short- to Medium-Term Production Forecasts

For the short to medium term (from the present to 5 years hence), outlooks have been developed based upon projected trends that could affect existing production facilities, planned expansions of existing facilities, and planned new facilities that operating companies, consortia, or Governments have projected to come online within indicated timeframes. The outlooks are not forecasts of what production will be but rather what the industry is likely to be able to produce given announced industry intentions.

3.2.1.1. Bauxite

The outlooks for the production of bauxite in Africa, the Middle East, the Americas, Asia, and Europe and Eurasia presented in table 12 are based on those in the summary chapters of MYB 2007 (Fong-Sam and others, 2009; Anderson and others, 2010; Levine and others, 2010; Mobbs and others, 2010; Yager and others, 2010). The summary chapters contain outlooks for individual bauxite-producing countries. African production is forecast to increase to 24 Mt in 2015 from 20 Mt in 2006; production from the Middle East is forecast to increase by almost 29 percent per year to 4.9 Mt in 2015 from 0.5 Mt in 2006. Aluminum production in the Americas is expected to reach 60 Mt in 2015, which is up from 50 Mt in 2006. Asia is expected to produce 160 Mt of bauxite, which represents an increase of almost 5 percent per year from 104 Mt. Bauxite production in Europe and Eurasia is expected to increase to 18 Mt in 2015 from 8.7 Mt in 2006. In total, global bauxite production is expected to increase by 4.4 percent per year to 270 Mt in 2015 from 183 Mt in 2006.

Table 12. Short- to medium-term (1- to 5-year) outlook for bauxite production.

[Data are in thousand metric tons. Totals may not add owing to independent rounding. Data are from USGS Minerals Yearbook 2007, v. III]

Region	2011	2013	2015
Africa	18,000	21,000	24,000
Americas	59,000	58,000	60,000
Asia and the Pacific	140,000	150,000	160,000
Europe and Eurasia	16,000	17,000	18,000
Middle East	1,600	4,900	4,900
World total	235,000	250,000	270,000

3.2.1.2. Aluminum

The outlooks for the production of aluminum in Africa, the Middle East, Asia, and Europe and Eurasia presented in table 13 are taken directly from four summary chapters of MYB 2007 (Fong-Sam and others, 2009; Levine and others, 2010; Mobbs and others, 2010; Yager and others, 2010); the outlooks for the Americas are based upon those presented in Anderson and others (2010) but have been modified to include data for the United States. If economic conditions warrant, there is expected to be sufficient industry capacity to produce 55 Mt of aluminum worldwide in 2011, 60 Mt in 2013, and 61 Mt in 2015. This represents an average rate of increase of 2.6 percent per year. The regions with the largest projected rates of increase are Africa (8.4 percent) and the Middle East (2.8 percent). The increase in Africa is expected to take place mainly in South Africa. The increase will be contingent upon the availability of sufficient power; South Africa has experienced power shortages in recent years. The increases in the Middle East are projected to spread across more countries, with Iran, Saudi Arabia, and the United Arab Emirates all slated for increases in aluminum production capacity. Bauxite production is expected to increase by almost 3 percent from 2011 to 2015 with production increases slated for Australia, Brazil, China, Guinea, India, Saudi Arabia, Sierra Leone, and Vietnam.

Table 13. Short- to medium-term (1- to 5-year) outlook for aluminum production.

[Data are in thousand metric tons. Totals may not add owing to independent rounding. Data are from USGS Minerals Yearbook 2007, v. III]

Region	2011	2013	2015
Africa	2,100	2,800	2,900
Americas	16,500	18,500	18,000
Asia	24,200	26,000	27,000
Europe and Eurasia	12,000	13,000	13,000
Middle East	4,270	5,395	5,395
World total	55,000	60,000	61,000

3.2.2. Long-Term Production Forecasts

Long-term forecasts of aluminum are made using a logistic regression model that relates aluminum consumption per capita to the average income in the country as measured by GDP per capita. The model estimates future consumption; assuming that the market for aluminum is in balance or nearly so, the production of aluminum can be inferred. Studies by DeYoung and Menzie (1999) and Menzie, DeYoung, and Steblez (2001) investigated the relationship of industrial consumption of metals, such as aluminum and copper, and noted that consumption was low when the average income was low but grew rapidly with increasing income until a threshold level of per capita consumption was reached. Menzie, Singer, and DeYoung (2005) and Singer and Menzie (2009) used a logistic regression, which captures the relationship between GDP per capita and metal consumption that was noted by DeYoung and Menzie (1999) and Menzie, DeYoung, and Steblez (2001), to estimate the per capita consumption of copper as a function of GDP per capita. They used projected economic growth rates and projected rates of population growth to estimate future GDP per capita.

3.2.2.1. The Model for Forecasting Long-Term Aluminum Consumption

Initial models of GDP per capita and aluminum consumption per capita were fit for the 40 most populous countries in the world (table 14). Figure 21 is a plot of those data. The initial model was not very satisfactory because France and the United Kingdom consume aluminum per capita at lower rates than is typical for other high-income countries. France and especially the United Kingdom have had falling rates of industrial consumption of metals in recent years as economic integration has increased among EU member states and as manufacturing has moved to other EU countries. Consumption in Italy and Spain has increased as it has declined in France and the United Kingdom. Therefore, the six large countries that were members of the EU were combined into one entity (EU6) for the purpose of fitting a logistic model to GDP per capita and aluminum consumption.

Table 14. Gross domestic product (GDP), population, aluminum consumption, per capita GDP, and aluminum consumption per capita for the 40 most populous countries in 2006.

Country	Population, in millions	GDP, in million dollars	Aluminum consumption, in million metric tons	GDP per capita, in dollars	Aluminum consumption per capita, in million metric tons
China	1,300	$2,630	8,650	$6,300	6.63
India	1,110	887	1,080	3,400	0.98
United States	298	13,200	9,170	42,000	30.70
Indonesia	232	364	288	3,700	1.24
Brazil	192	1,070	1,040	8,400	5.45
Pakistan	166	129	34	2,400	0.21
Bangladesh	150	65	24	2,100	0.16
Russia	142	979	1,050	10,700	7.37
Nigeria	140	115	11	1,000	0.08
Japan	128	4,370	3,390	30,700	26.60
Mexico	107	840	725	10,100	6.75
Philippines	95	117	26	5,100	0.28
Vietnam	85	61	88	3,000	1.03
Germany	82	2,900	2,620	29,800	31.80
Ethiopia	77	74	0	800	0.00
Egypt	74	107	110	4,400	1.48
Turkey	74	392	433	7,900	5.88
Iran	65	212	168	8,100	2.59
Thailand	65	206	407	8,300	6.29
France	63	2,230	945	30,000	14.90
Congo (Kinshasa)	62	19	0	800	0.00
United Kingdom	61	2,370	567	30,900	9.35
Italy	58	1,850	1,690	28,400	29.00
Republic of Korea	49	888	1,150	20,400	23.50
South Africa	48	257	264	12,100	5.51
Burma	47	13	0	1,600	0.00
Ukraine	47	106	39	6,800	0.84
Colombia	42	136	77	7,100	1.83
Spain	40	1,230	863	25,200	21.40
Argentina	40	213	146	13,700	3.68
Sudan	39	36	1	2,100	0.02
Tanzania	39	14	0	700	0.00
Poland	39	342	227	12,700	5.88
Kenya	36	23	13	1,200	0.36
Algeria	33	115	6	7,200	0.18
Canada	33	1,280	1,030	32,900	31.50
Morocco	30	65	12	4,300	0.40
Uganda	29	10	0	1,700	0.01
Peru	28	93	2	6,100	0.07
Nepal	28	9	0	1,500	0.00

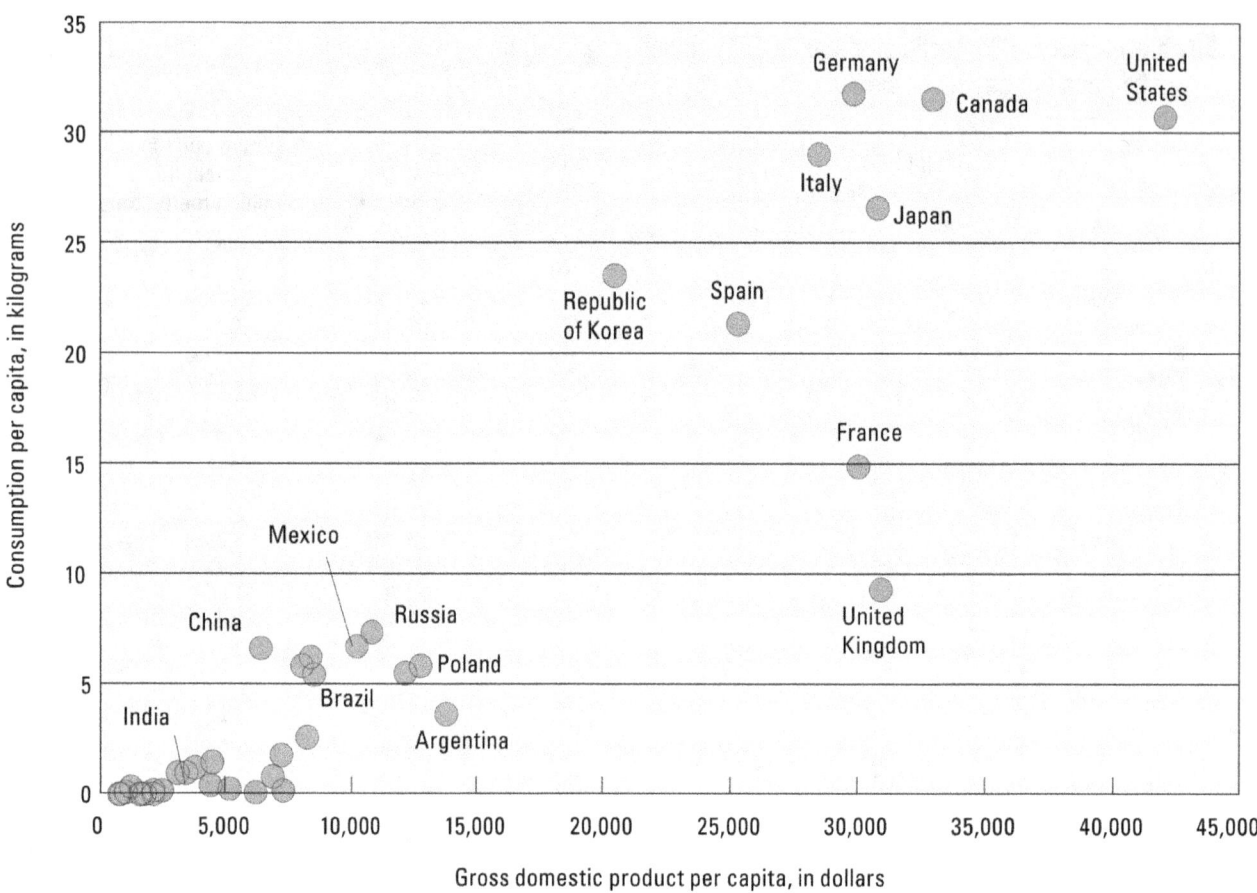

Figure 21. Graph showing aluminum consumption per capita against purchasing power parity gross domestic product per capita in 2006.

Figure 22 shows a plot of the EU6 and the other 34 populous countries' aluminum consumption per capita versus GDP per capita and the logistic equation and curve fit to the data. All the parameters of the equation are significantly different from zero at a 5 percent confidence level and the curve provides a reasonable approximation of the data, albeit with significant error. The error indicates that items beyond income affect aluminum consumption per capita. The model of consumption is essentially projective based upon assumed rates of economic growth. Nevertheless, the model is likely to give a reasonable status quo projection of aluminum consumption into the future.

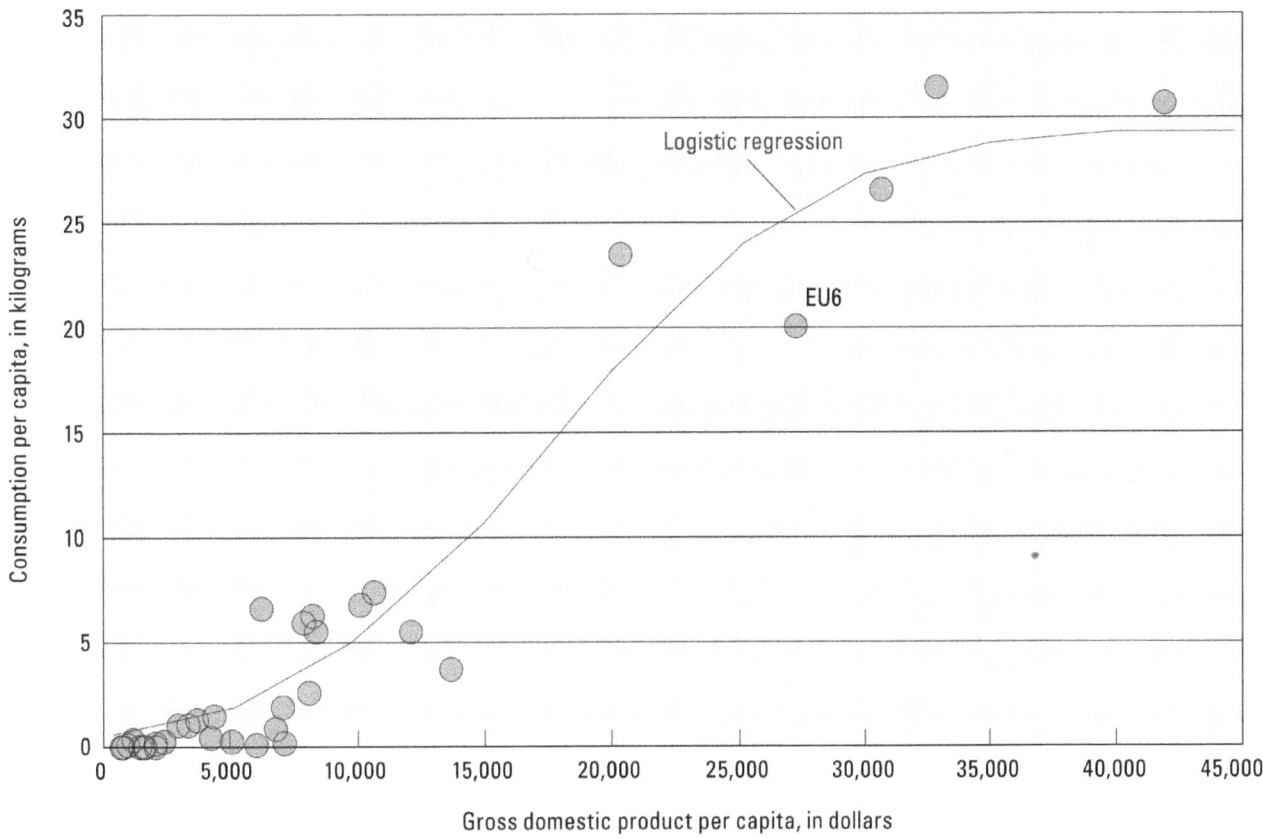

Figure 22. Graph showing aluminum consumption per capita against purchasing power parity gross domestic product per capita in 2006 [includes the six largest member states of the European Union (EU6)]. For the logistic regression, aluminum consumption per capita was calculated from the following equation:

$$\frac{29.41}{1+e^{(-0.00021*(x-17,000))}},$$

where x is the gross domestic product per capita.

3.2.3. Forecasts

Table 15 presents forecasts for 2015, 2020, and 2025 for the population, GDP per capita, aluminum consumption per capita, and aluminum consumption for the 20 most populous countries in 2006. Growth rates are based on the average of the past 10 years. The table also uses the ratio of the aluminum consumption in the 20 most populous countries to global aluminum production to estimate world aluminum consumption. If it is assumed that aluminum production is equal to aluminum consumption, then the estimates can be used to examine a number of implications of the model.

Table 15. Estimated population, purchasing power parity gross domestic product per capita, aluminum consumption per capita, and aluminum consumption for 2015, 2020, and 2025.

[GDPpp/c, purchasing power parity gross domestic product per capita; Al/c, aluminum consumption per capita; XX, not applicable]

Country	2015				2020				2025			
	Population, in millions	GDPpp/c, in dollars	Al/c, in kilograms	Aluminum consumption, in thousand metric tons	Population, in millions	GDPpp/c, in dollars	Al/c, in kilograms	Aluminum consumption, in thousand metric tons	Population, in millions	GDPpp/c, in dollars	Al/c, in kilograms	Aluminum consumption, in thousand metric tons
China	1,400	13,900	8.86	12,400	1,430	21,800	20.90	29,900	1,450	34,600	28.70	41,700
India	1,290	5,350	1.82	2,360	1,370	7,100	2.60	3,560	1,430	9,520	4.17	5,970
United States	332	49,300	29.40	9,750	346	54,800	29.40	10,200	359	61,200	29.40	10,600
Indonesia	244	5,000	1.70	414	254	5,850	2.02	513	263	6,870	2.48	654
Brazil	203	10,300	4.86	986	209	11,600	6.14	1,280	214	13,200	7.94	1,700
Pakistan	206	3,000	1.12	230	226	3,490	1.24	280	246	4,100	1.40	345
Bangladesh	175	2,790	1.07	187	186	3,350	1.20	223	195	4,080	1.40	273
Russia	138	18,600	16.20	2,230	135	25,500	24.90	3,360	132	34,900	28.70	3,790
Nigeria	176	1,470	0.80	142	193	1,880	0.88	169	210	2,420	0.98	207
Japan	126	37,100	29.00	3,650	124	41,700	29.30	3,630	121	47,100	29.40	3,550
Mexico	116	12,200	6.75	784	120	13,700	8.58	1,030	123	15,500	11.20	1,370
Philippines	102	6,570	2.34	238	110	7,410	2.77	305	117	8,480	3.42	400
Vietnam	94	5,030	1.71	160	98	6,740	2.42	237	102	9,080	3.84	392
Germany	81	36,100	28.90	2,350	80	40,300	29.20	2,350	79	45,100	29.30	2,330
Ethiopia	96	1,090	0.74	71	108	1,300	0.78	84	120	1,560	0.82	98
Egypt	92	5,510	1.88	173	99	6,550	2.33	230	105	7,850	3.02	317
Turkey	80	12,300	6.86	549	84	15,700	11.50	965	87	20,200	18.60	1,620
Iran	80	10,300	4.80	382	84	12,500	7.05	590	87	15,300	10.90	947
Thailand	70	11,900	6.44	450	71	14,900	10.30	735	73	18,700	16.30	1,180
France	64	35,500	28.80	1,840	65	38,600	29.10	1,890	66	42,000	29.30	1,930
Total for selected countries				39,300				61,500				79,300
World total				58,700				91,900				119,000

52

The model is quite simple and does not provide associated confidence limits or address possible affects of important variables, such as price and substitution. Errors associated with the long term are necessarily large as errors are typically multiplicative, enlarging upon previous errors. Prices are a nonlinear function of the balance between the supply and demand for a commodity. Because mine and plant capacities at the various steps in the aluminum production process are capital intensive and benefit from economies of scale, mine and plant capacities are typically added, or enlarged, in large increments that require time to build. As a result, supply is relatively inelastic with regards to increases in demand beyond the point of installed capacity. Therefore, forecasting prices is very difficult even for the near term. Evaluation of substitution requires comparison of price and performance measures for competing materials, such as composite materials. An evaluation of such materials is beyond the scope of this study.

World aluminum consumption, which was 45.3 Mt in 2006, is estimated to be 59 Mt in 2015, 92 Mt in 2020, and 120 Mt in 2025. Most of the increases are estimated to occur in low- and middle-income countries. Notably, the BRIC countries (Brazil, Russia, India, and China), which accounted for 26 percent of world consumption in 2006, are expected to account for 31 percent of world consumption in 2015, 42 percent of world consumption in 2020, and 45 percent of world consumption in 2025. Consumption by the United States, Japan, Germany and France, which was 16.1 Mt in 2006 (36 percent of world consumption), is estimated to be 18 Mt in 2025 (15 percent of world consumption).

4. Conclusions

A number of important conclusions can be reached based upon this study. The conclusions are organized by the section of the report on which they are based to allow easy access to information related to the formation of the conclusions.

4.1. Methods of Present Study (2.3)

A focus on changes in mineral consumption as countries experience economic growth and a rise in income (GDP per capita) can yield important insights into dynamic material flows.

4.2. Macro-Level Flows (3.1.1)

Macro-level flows estimated by this study for bauxite production, alumina production, and primary aluminum production are similar to those calculated by the IAI for 2006.

Secondary aluminum production estimated by this study was significantly lower than that estimated by the IAI for 2006. In addition, the ratio of post-consumer to total scrap estimated by the USGS (Papp, 2009) for the United States differs significantly from the IAI estimate of that ratio for the world.

4.3. Micro-Level Flows (3.1.2)

The European model of alumina refineries and aluminum smelters presented in this section of the report demonstrates that the application of existing technologies could reduce byproduct wastes produced as a result of aluminum production.

Ongoing research is identifying uses for some wastes such as "red mud." These uses could significantly reduce some wastes from aluminum production.

Reduction of GHGs from aluminum production is under the control of two groups. PFCs and CO_2 generated from fuel use and reduction processes are under the control of the producer of the aluminum. GHGs generated to produce the electricity used by aluminum producers are under the control of the owners of the electrical grid.

4.4. Consumption (3.1.3)

In high-income countries, such as Germany, Japan, and the United States, aluminum consumption per capita is either growing very slowly or is not growing. In a few countries in the European Union, such as France and the United Kingdom, economic integration and relocation of industries have led to a decrease in aluminum consumption.

Aluminum consumption per capita increases rapidly to about 20 kilograms per person from 2 kilograms per person as per capita income increases to $20,000 from $5,000.

The end uses to which aluminum is put appear to differ significantly between high-income countries and low- and middle-income countries. In low- and middle-income countries, the main uses of aluminum are in electrical systems and construction. In high-income countries, the leading use of aluminum is in transportation. Inconsistent end-use classifications, however, limit the quantification of these differences.

Because of the long in-service times of electrical systems and buildings and other construction, recycling of significant amounts of post-consumer scrap is unlikely to begin in the countries that are currently experiencing rapid economic growth until 2020 to 2025.

Recycling rates of used beverage cans can be high in low- and middle-income countries owing to the availability of low wages for labor; however, the amount of material going into packaging is relatively small in these countries.

As shown for light vehicles, production data for goods can be combined with intensity of use data to estimate material in use. When these data are combined with estimates of aluminum shipments and the in-service life of the good, it is possible to estimate the contribution of that type of good to new and post-consumer scrap. For example, the manufacture of light vehicles generates relatively small volumes of new aluminum scrap from fabricators and manufacturers. In contrast, commercial aircraft manufacturing generates almost 1 t of new scrap for each ton of material in an aircraft.

4.5. Future Global Mass Flows of Aluminum (3.2)

4.5.1. Short- to Medium-Term Forecasts (3.2.1)

Based upon announced production plans, the capacity of bauxite mines is expected to increase to 270 Mt by 2015 from 183 Mt in 2006. This represents an almost 48 percent increase over 2006. Major increases in mine capacity are expected in Australia, China, Brazil, India, Saudi Arabia, Russia, and Guinea, in order of the size of the capacity increase.

Future aluminum production capacity based upon announced production plans is expected to reach 61 Mt in 2015 from 45.3 Mt in 2006. This represents an increase of almost 3.4 percent per year. The largest increases are expected to take place in China, Brazil, the United Arab Emirates, Canada, India, South Africa, Saudi Arabia, and Qatar, in order of the size of the capacity increase.

4.5.2. Long-Term Forecasts (3.2.2)

Based on a model relating consumption to income, aluminum consumption by 2025 is likely to be 120 Mt compared with 45.3 Mt in 2006. This represents a growth rate of 4.1 percent per year. Most of the increased consumption will take place in countries that consumed only modest amounts of aluminum in 2006. China, which consumed about 6.6 kg per capita in 2006, is expected to consume 28.7 kg per capita in 2025. Russia, which consumed 7.4 kg per capita in 2006, is expected to consume 28.7 kg per capita in 2025, and Brazil, which consumed 5.5 kg per capita in 2006, is expected to consume 7.9 kg per capita in 2025. Brazil's consumption is based on a relatively modest projection that its rate of economic growth will be only 3 percent per year; recent data indicate that Brazil's future rate of growth could be greater than 3 percent. India, which consumed 1.8 kg per capita in 2006, is expected to consume 4.2 kg per capita in 2025. Consumption in high-income countries is not expected to rise significantly on a per capita basis, but total consumption may increase modestly owing to population increases.

4.5.3. Implications of the Forecasts (3.2.3)

To meet a consumption of 120 Mt of aluminum, the world will need to produce about 570 Mt of bauxite and about 230 Mt of alumina. This production will generate significant levels of wastes even if technological improvements are made to current production processes.

A key question related to this increased consumption will be what portion of the consumption is satisfied by primary aluminum and what portion is from secondary aluminum, as this will have a considerable influence on the amount of GHGs generated by aluminum production. That portion of secondary aluminum that comes from new scrap is likely to increase proportionately with overall consumption. The data on changing patterns of end use with increased income suggest, however, that at least initially, the proportion of aluminum that is generated from old scrap may decrease as countries undergoing economic growth initially use aluminum mainly to add to infrastructure that has long terms of in-service use. Later, as these countries continue to experience economic growth, they are likely to increase the amount of aluminum they consume in transportation end uses. As this takes place, recycling of post-consumer scrap will rise but the timing of the increase will be governed by the mix of transportation and the in-service terms of individual modes of transportation. China and India are increasing their use of vehicles at a very rapid rate; if the in-service terms of the vehicles are 10 to 12 years, then post-consumer scrap from this increase is not likely to appear until sometime between 2020 and 2025. Rates of recycling of used beverage cans are typically high in low- to middle-income countries; however, the amount of material recovered is likely to remain modest as the volume of such material will remain at low levels for most of the period of the forecast.

If the proportion of aluminum production that comes from primary smelters increases, at least until 2025, a reduction in GHGs must come from increases in the efficiency of aluminum smelters or in reduced use of fossil fuels for generation of the electricity used in aluminum production. The magnitude of the increases in aluminum consumption suggests that both gains in efficiency and switching of fuel sources will need to be substantial just to maintain emissions at the current level.

5. References Cited

Airbus S.A.S., 2007, Airbus 2006 results: Airbus S.A.S. press release, January 17, accessed June 15, 2010, at *http://www.airbus.com/en/presscentre/pressreleases/press-release/ ?tx_ttnews%5Bswords%5D=2006%20results&tx_ttnews%5Btt_news%5D=440&tx_ttnews%5Bback Pid%5D=1765&cHash=3abca17aca.*

Airliners.net, 2010, Aircraft technical data and specifications: Airliners.net, accessed June 15, 2010, at *http://www.airliners.net/aircraft-data/.*

Alcoa Inc., 2009, Alcoa unloads first bauxite shipment from Juruti in Alumar refinery, in São Luís–MA: Alcoa Inc. press release, October 9, accessed March 10, 2009, at *http://www.alcoa.com/brazil/en/news/releases/2009_10_09.asp?initSection=1000.*

Anderson, S.T., Bermúdez-Lugo, Omayra, Gurmendi, A.C., Perez, A.A., Wacaster, Susan, Wallace, G.J., and Wilburn, D.R, 2010, The mineral industries of Latin America and Canada, *in* Area reports— International—Latin America and Canada: U.S. Geological Survey Minerals Yearbook 2007, v. III, p. 1.1–1.34, accessed June 15, 2010, at *http://minerals.usgs.gov/minerals/pubs/country/2007/ myb3-sum-2007-latin-canada.pdf.*

Aslam, M., Khalil, K., Rasmussen, R.A., Culbertson, J.A., Prins, J.M., Grimsrud, E.P., and Shearer, M.J., 2003, Atmospheric perfluorocarbons: Environmental Science and Technology, v. 37, no. 19, October, p. 4358–61. (Also available at *http://dx.doi.org/10.1021/es030327a.*)

Associação Brasileira do Alumínio, [undated], Domestic consumption of aluminum products by end use—2008: Associação Brasileira do Alumínio, accessed October 15, 2010, at *http://www.abal.org.br/english/industria/estatisticas_consdomsetor.asp.*

Aviation Today, 2007, Bombardier deliveries down, t-props up: Aviation Today, February 27, accessed June 15, 2010, at *http://www.aviationtoday.com/ran/topstories/ Bombardier-Deliveries-Down-T-Props-Up_8971.html.*

BCS, Inc., 2007, U.S. energy requirements for aluminum production—Historical perspective, theoretical limits and current practices: U.S. Department of Energy, February, accessed April 23, 2010, at *http://www1.eere.energy.gov/industry/aluminum/pdfs/al_theoretical.pdf.*

Beck, T.R., 2008, Electrolytic production of aluminum, *in* Nagy, Zoltan, ed., Electrochemistry encyclopedia: Cleveland, Ohio, Ernest B. Yeager Center for Electrochemical Sciences (YCES) and the Chemical Engineering Department, Case Western Reserve University, available at *http://electrochem.cwru.edu/encycl/art-a01-al-prod.htm.*

Boin, U.M.J., and Bertram, M., 2005, Melting standardized aluminum scrap—A mass balance model for Europe: Journal of Metals, v. 57, no. 8, August, p. 26–33.

Boltramovich, Sergey, Dudarev, Grigory, and Gorelov, Vladimir, 2003, The melting iron curtain—A competitive analysis of the Northwest Russian metal cluster: Helsinki, Finland, The Research Institute of the Finnish Economy, Taloustieto Oy, 138 p.

Bray, E.L., 2010a, Aluminum, *in* Metals and minerals: U.S. Geological Survey Minerals Yearbook 2008, v. I, p. 5.1–5.19, accessed October 14, 2010, at *http://minerals.usgs.gov/minerals/pubs/ commodity/aluminum/myb1-2008-alumi.pdf.*

Bray, E.L., 2010b, Bauxite and alumina, *in* Metals and minerals: U.S. Geological Survey Minerals Yearbook 2008, v. I, p. 10.1–10.11, accessed October 14, 2010, at *http://minerals.usgs.gov/minerals/ pubs/commodity/bauxite/myb1-2008-bauxi.pdf.*

Carbon Emitters, 2009, Do nickel producers emit a lot of carbon?: Carbon Emitters, written blog commun., November 26, accessed February 22, 2010, at *http://www.carbonemitters.org/.*

Chen, Weiqiang, Shi, Lei, Qian, Li, 2009, Substance flow analysis of aluminium in mainland China for 2001, 2004, and 2007—Exploring its initial sources, eventual sinks and the pathways linking them: Resources, Conservation and Recycling, v. 64, issue 9, July, p. 557–570.

CiDRA Minerals Processing, Inc., 2010, CiDRA minerals processing—Alumina refining process solutions: Wallingford, Conn., CiDRA Minerals Processing, Inc. brochure, 4 p., accessed February 2, 2010, at *http://www.cidra.com/document_library/BI0349_Alumina_Brochure.pdf.*

DeYoung, J.H., Jr., and Menzie, W.D., 1999, The changing uses of mineral information—A government perspective, *in* Otto, James, and Hyo-Sun, Kim, eds., Proceedings of the workshop on the sustainable development of non-renewable resources toward the 21st century, New York, N.Y., October 15–16, 1998: New York, United Nations Development Programme, p. 111–127.

Ducker Worldwide, LLC, 2008, 2009 update on North American light vehicle aluminum content compared to the other countries and regions of the world—Phase II: Troy, Mich., Ducker Worldwide, LLC presentation, 96 slides, accessed at *http://aluminumintransportation.org/downloads/ Ducker%20International%20Final%20Report%202009%20-%20II.pdf.*

Empresa Brasileira de Aeronáutica S.A., 2007, Embraer reports fourth-quarter 2006 deliveries and total company backlog; São José dos Campos, Brazil, Empresa Brasileira de Aeronáutica S.A. press release, January 15, 7 p. (Also available at *http://www.embraer.com.br/institucional/download/ 2_002-Ins-VPF-Deliveries_4Q2006-I-06.pdf.*)

European Aluminium Association, 2008, Environmental profile report for the European aluminium industry: European Aluminium Association, April, 12 p., accessed February 4, 2010, at *http://www.eaa.net/upl/4/en/doc/EAA_Environmental_profile_report_May08.pdf.*

Fong-Sam, Yolanda, Kuo, C.S., Shi, Lin, Tse, Pui-Kwan, Wacaster, Susan, Wilburn, D.R., and Wu, J.C., 2009, The mineral industries of Asia and the Pacific, *in* Area reports—International—Asia and the Pacific: U.S. Geological Survey Minerals Yearbook 2007, v. III, p. 1.1–1.34. (Also available at *http://minerals.usgs.gov/minerals/pubs/country/2007/myb3-sum-2007-asia-pacific.pdf.*)

Fraser, P., Trudinger, C., Dunse, B., Krummel, P, and Steele, P., 2009, PFC emissions from Australian & global aluminum production: 2009 ESRL Global Monitoring Annual Conference, Boulder, Colorado, May 13-14, 2009, Presentation, 27 p., accessed February 4, 2010, at *http://www.esrl.noaa.gov/gmd/publications/annmeet2009/presentations/4-Fraser.pdf.*

Fraunhofer Institute for Systems and Innovations Research, 2009, Methodology for the free allocation of emission allowances in the EU ETS post 2012—Sector report for the aluminum industry: Study Contract: 07.0307/2008/515770/ETU/C2, Ecofys project no. PECSNL082164, 21 p., accessed May 7, 2010, at *http://ec.europa.eu/environment/climat/emission/pdf/bm/BM study - Aluminium.pdf.*

FreightCar America, Inc., [undated], Coal and coke cars: FreightCar America, Inc., accessed February 2, 2010, at *http://www.freightcaramerica.com/Coke-Coal-Railcars.htm.*

FreightCar America, Inc., 2007, Annual report for 2006: Chicago, Ill., FreightCar America, Inc., 69 p.

Grishayev, S.I., and Petrov, I.M., 2008, The ratio of primary and secondary raw material in non-ferrous metal production in Russia: Mineral Resources of Russia, v. 5, p. 17–23.

Hatayama, Hiroki, Yamada, Hiroyuki, Daigo, Ichiro, Matsuno, Yasunari, Adachi, Yoshihiro, 2007, Dynamic substance flow analysis of aluminum and its alloying elements: Materials Transactions, v. 48, no. 9, p. 2518–2524.

Indian Bureau of Mines, 2008, Indian Minerals Yearbook 2007: Nagpur, India, Indian Bureau of Mines, 1,038 p.

International Aluminium Institute, 2003, The aluminum sector greenhouse gas protocol—Greenhouse gas emissions monitoring and reporting by the aluminum industry: International Aluminium Institute, October, 65 p., accessed February 2, 2010, at *http://www.world-aluminium.org/cache/fl0000127.pdf.*

International Aluminium Institute, 2007, Life cycle assessment of aluminum—Inventory data for the primary aluminum industry, year 2005 update: London, United Kingdom, International Aluminium Institute, 42 p.

International Aluminium Institute, 2009a, Aluminium for future generations—2009 update: International Aluminium Institute, 7 p., accessed February 2, 2010, at *http://www.world-aluminium.org/cache/fl0000303.pdf*.

International Aluminium Institute, 2009b, Fourth sustainable bauxite mining report—IV2008: International Aluminium Institute, 16 p., accessed February 25, 2010, at *http://www.world-aluminium.org/cache/fl0000292.pdf*.

International Aluminium Institute, 2009c, Results of the 2008 anode effect survey—Report on the aluminum industry's global perfluorocarbon gases emissions reduction programme: International Aluminium Institute, August 24, 44 p., accessed February 4, 2010, at *http://www.world-aluminium.org/cache/fl0000300.pdf*.

International Aluminium Institute, 2010, About aluminum—Applications and products—Transportation—Aerospace: International Aluminium Institute, accessed February 4, 2010, at *http://www.world-aluminium.org/About+Aluminium/Applications+and+Products/Transportation/Aerospace/*.

International Organization of Motor Vehicle Manufacturers, 2007, 2006 production statistics: International Organization of Motor Vehicle Manufacturers, accessed October 15, 2010, at *http://www.oica.net/category/production-statistics/2006-statistics/*.

Jet Information Services, Inc., [undated], World jet inventory—Aviation statistics: Jet Information Services, Inc., accessed June 15, 2010, via *http://www.jetinventory.com/*.

Levine, R.M., Brininstool, Mark, Anderson, S.T., Newman, H.R., Perez, A.A., Wallace, G.J., and Wilburn, D.R., 2010, The mineral industries of Europe and Central Eurasia, *in* Area reports—International—Europe and Central Eurasia: U.S. Geological Survey Minerals Yearbook 2007, v. III, p. 1.1–1.49, accessed June 15, 2010, at *http://minerals.usgs.gov/minerals/pubs/country/2007/myb3-sum-2007-europe-eurasia.pdf*.

Martchek, Kenneth, 2006, Modelling more sustainable aluminium: International Journal of Life Cycle Assessment, v. 11, no. 1, p. 34–37. (Also available at *http://dx.doi.org/10.1065/lca2006.01.231*.)

Martchek, Kenneth, [2007], Aluminum mass flow modeling and emissions projections: International Aluminium Institute presentation, 17 slides. (Also available at *https://www.iea.org/work/2007/aluminium/martchek.pdf*.)

Menzie, W.D., DeYoung, J.H., Jr., and Steblez, W.G., 2001, Some implications of changing patterns of mineral consumption: U.S. Geological Survey Open-File Report 03–382, accessed June 15, 2010, at *http://pubs.usgs.gov/of/2003/of03-382/of03-382.html*.

Menzie, W.D., Singer, D.A., and DeYoung, J.H., Jr., 2005, Mineral resources and consumption in the 21st century, chap. 2 *of* Simpson, R.D., Toman, M.A., and Ayres, R.U., eds., Scarcity and growth revisited—Natural resources and the environment in the new millennium: Washington, D.C., Resources for the Future, p. 33–53.

Metals Advisor, 2010, Aluminum competitive issues—Environmental issues: Metals Advisor, accessed May 7, 2010, at *http://www.energysolutionscenter.org/heattreat/metalsadvisor/aluminum/industry_overview/competitive_issues/environmental_issues.htm*.

Mobbs, P.M., Wallace, G.J., Wilburn, D.R., Taib, Mowafa, and Yager, T.R., 2010, The mineral industries of the Middle East, *in* Area reports—International—Africa and the Middle East: U.S. Geological Survey Minerals Yearbook 2007, v. III, p. 42.1–42.12 (Also available at *http://minerals.usgs.gov/minerals/pubs/country/2007/myb3-sum-2007-middle-east.pdf*.)

Nagy, Zoltan, ed., 2010, Electrochemistry enclyclopedia: Ernest B. Yeager Center for Electrochemical Sciences and the Chemical Engineering Department, Case Western Reserve University, accessed October 15, 2010, at *http://electrochem.cwru.edu/encycl/*.

Papp, J.F., 2009, Recycling—Metals, *in* Metals and minerals: U.S. Geological Survey 2007, v. I, p. 61.1–61.6. (Also available at *http://minerals.usgs.gov/minerals/pubs/commodity/recycle/ myb1-2007-recyc.pdf* .)

Plunkert, P.A., 2006, Aluminum recycling in the United States in 2000: U.S. Geological Survey Circular 1196-W, 11 p., accessed February 2, 2010, at *http://pubs.usgs.gov/circ/c1196w/*. (Supersedes USGS Open-File Report 2005–1051.)

Pontikes, Y., 2005a, Red mud—Production: Red Mud Project, July 13, accessed March 8, 2010, at *http://www.redmud.org/Production.html*.

Pontikes, Y., 2005b, Red mud—Characteristic: Red Mud Project, May 2, accessed March 8, 2010, at *http://www.redmud.org/Characteristics.html*.

Pontikes, Y., 2005c, Red mud—Disposal: Red Mud Project, April 22, accessed March 8, 2010, at *http://www.redmud.org/Disposal.html*.

Pontikes, Y., 2005d, Red mud—Applications: Red Mud Project, March 14, accessed March 8, 2010, at *http://www.redmud.org/Applications.html*.

Pontikes, Y., 2005e, Red mud—Industrial uses: Red Mud Project, March 14, accessed March 8, 2010, at *http://www.redmud.org/Industrial_Uses.html*.

Rosenqvist, Terkel, 2004, Principles of extractive metallurgy: Trondheim, Norway, Tapir Academic Press, 506 p.

Royal Boskalis Westminster NV, 2010, The Berbice River project: Royal Boskalis Westminster NV project data sheet, 2 p., accessed March 3, 2010, at *http://www.boskalis.nl/ media/downloads/nl_NL/Projecten/Zuid%20Amerika/berbice_river_jan_2010_lr.pdf*.

Simmonds, P.G., Greally, B.R., Olivier, S., Nickless, G., Cooke, K.M.., and Dietz, R.N., 2002, The background atmospheric concentrations of cyclic perfluorocarbon tracers determined by negative ion-chemical ionization mass spectrometry: Atmospheric Environment, v. 36, issue 13, May, p. 2147–2156, accessed February 4, 2010, at *http://dx.doi.org/10.1016/S1352-2310(02)00194-2*.

Singer, D.A., and Menzie, W.D., 2009, Patterns in industrial copper consumption [abs.]: Geological Society of America Abstracts with Programs, v. 41, no. 7, p. 610.

The Boeing Company, 2010, Orders and deliveries: The Boeing Company, accessed June 15, 2010, at *http://active.boeing.com/commercial/orders/index.cfm*.

U.S. Environmental Protection Agency, 2006, High GWP gases and climate change: U.S. Environmental Protection Agency, accessed February 3, 2010, at *http://www.epa.gov/highgwp/ scientific.html*.

U.S. Geological Survey, 2010a, Area reports—International: U.S. Geological Survey Minerals Yearbook 2007, v. III, 1,013 p.

U.S. Geological Survey, 2010,, Metals and minerals: U.S. Geological Survey Minerals Yearbook 2007, v. III, 1,070 p.

Yager, T.R., Bermúdez-Lugo, Omayra, Mobbs, P.M., Newman, H.R., Wallace, G.J., and Wilburn, D.R., 2010, The mineral industries of Africa, *in* Area reports—International—Africa and the Middle East: U.S. Geological Survey Minerals Yearbook 2007, v. III, p. 1.1–1.26. (Also available at *http://minerals.usgs.gov/minerals/pubs/country/2007/myb3-sum-2007-africa.pdf*.)

6. Appendixes

Appendix 1. Global bauxite mines in 2007.

[km, kilometer; e, estimated; NA, not available]

Major operating company	Location	Annual capacity[1]
Australia		
Baddington open pit bauxite mine {Worsley Alumina Pty. Ltd., manager [BHP Billiton Ltd., 86%; Japan Alumina Associates (Australia) Pty. Ltd., 10%; Sojitz Alumina Pty. Ltd., 4%]}	50 km northeast of Collie, Western Australia	13,200
Gove open pit bauxite mine (Rio Tinto Alcan, 100%)	Gove Peninsula, Northern Territory	8,000
Huntly open pit bauxite mine (Alcoa World Alumina Australia, 100%)	80 km south of Perth, Western Australia	20,000
Weipa-Andoom open pit bauxite mine [Comalco Ltd., operator (Rio Tinto plc, 100%)]	Weipa, Queensland	18,200
Willowdale open pit bauxite mine [Comalco Ltd., operator (Rio Tinto plc, 100%)]	130 km south of Perth, Western Australia	8,600
Azerbaijan		
Permian deposit	Nakhichevan region	NA
Bosnia and Herzegovina		
A.D. Boksit Milici	Mine at Milici	1,500
Energoinvest	Vlasenica	2,000
	Jajce	
	Bosanska Krupa	
	Posusje	
	Listica	
	Citluk	
Brazil		
Alcan Alumínio Poços de Caldas (Alucaldas) (Alcan Alumínio do Brasil S.A., 100%)	Pocos de Caldas, Minas Gerais State (mine)	1,000
Alcoa Alumínio S.A. (Alcoa Inc., 54%; BHP Billiton, 36%; Alcan Aluminum Ltd., 10%)	Pocos de Caldas, Minas Gerais State (mine)	400
Alumar Consortium S.A. (Alcoa Alumínio S.A., 100%)	Juriti bauxite mine, Para State	4,000
Companhia Brasileira de Alumínio (CBA) (Votorantim Group, 100%)	Mira Mine	5,000
CBA	Pocos de Caldas, Minas Gerais State (mine)	1,000
Consortium Paragominas S.A. [Vale S.A., 48.7%; Mineração Rio do Norte S.A. (MRN), 24.6%; Nippon Amazon Aluminum Co., 12.2%; Companhia Brasileira de Alumínio (CBA), 5.7%; others, 8.8%]	Jabuti, Para State (mine)	5,400
Mineração Rio do Norte S.A. (MRN) (Vale S.A., 40%; BHP Billiton plc, 14.8%; Alcoa Inc., 13.2%; Alcan Empreendimentos Ltda., 12%; Companhia Brasileira de Alumínio (CBA), 10%; Norsk Hydro Comercio e Industria, 5%; Reynolds Aluminio do Brasil, 5%)	Papagalo, Para State (mine)	2,000
MRN	Trombetas, Para State (mine)	2,000
MRN	Oriximina, Para State (mine)	14,500
Vale do Rio Doce and partners	Paragominas II	4,500
China		
Aluminum Corp. of China	Guangxi Huayin[2]	2,100
Aluminum Corp. of China	Nanchuan, Chongqing[3]	2,000
Dominican Republic		
Sierra Bauxita Dominicana S.A.	Pedernales region (under development)	NA
Ghana		
Ghana Bauxite Co. Ltd. (Alcan Aluminum Ltd., 80%, and Government, 20%)	Bauxite mine at Awaso	1,000

Appendix 1. Global bauxite mines in 2007.—Continued

[km, kilometer; e, estimated; NA, not available]

	Greece	
Delphi-Distomon S.A.; Hellenic Bauxites of Distomon S.A. (Aluminium de Grèce S.A.)	Delphi-Distomon mine, Voiotia and Fokida	500
Eleusis Bauxites Mines, S.A.	Plant in Aghia Marina	400
	Plant in Drama	
	Plant in Itea	
	Mine near Drama	
	Mine near Itea	
	Mine in Fthiotis and Fokida	
S&B Industrial Minerals, S.A. (Eliopoulos-Kyriakopoulos Group)	Mine at Fokida	2,000
	Plant at Fokida	
	Plant at Itea	
	Guinea	
Alumina Company of Guinea (United Company RUSAL, 100%)	Friguia Mine, Fria	2,800
Compagnie des Bauxites de Guinée (CBG) [Government, 49%, and Halco Mining Inc., 51% (Halco Mining was a consortium formed by Alcoa Inc., 45%; Alcan Inc., 45%; and Dadco Group, 10%)]	Kamsar	14,000
	Sangaredi	
Compagnie des Bauxites de Kindia (CBK) (United Company RUSAL, 100%)	Debele Mine, Kindia	3,000
	Guyana	
Aroaima Bauxite Co. (United Company RUSAL, 90%, and Government, 10%)	Kwakwani, East Berbice District[2]	2,000
Omai Bauxite Mining Inc. (Bosai Mining Co. Ltd., 70%, and Government of Guyana, 30%)	Omai Bauxite Mine and Processing Plant located close to Linden on the Demerara River about 100 kilometers south of Guyana's capital city of Georgetown[2]	1,500
	Hungary	
Magyar Aluminium Ltd. (MAL) (owns and operates Bakony Bauxite Mines Ltd.)	Bakony District, extending roughly 100 kilometers northeast along Lake Balaton	1,500
	India	
Bharat Aluminium Co. Ltd. (Indian Government, 49%, and Sterlite Industries Ltd., 51%)	Amarkantak Mine, Madhya Pradesh	200
Gujarat Mineral Development Corp. (Gujarat State government, 100%)	Kutch Mine, Gujarat	500
	Saurashtra Mine, Gujarat	
Hindalco Aluminium Co. Ltd. (Birla Group, 33%; foreign investors, 26%; private Indian investors, 23%; financial institutions, 18%)	Mines in Lohardaga District, Jharkhand	750
Hindalco Industries	Utkal[3]	3,000
Indian Aluminium Co. Ltd. [Indian interests, 60.4%, and Alcan Aluminium Ltd. (Canada), 39.6%]	Kolhapur district mines, Maharashtra	600
Indian Aluminium Co. Ltd.	Mines in Lohardaga District, Jharkhand	200
Minerals & Minerals Ltd. (Indian Government, 100%)	Mines in Richuguta, Palamau District, Jharkhand	200
National Aluminium Co. Ltd. (Indian Government, 100%)	Mines in Panchpatmali Hills, Koraput District, Orissa	4,800
	Indonesia	
PT Antam Tbk (Government, 65%)	Kijang, Bintan Island, Riau[2]	1,300
	Italy	
Sardabauxiti S.p.A. (Cogein S.p.A., 40%; Comtec S.p.A., 40%; Icofin Co., 20%)	Mine at Olmedo, Sardinia	350

Appendix 1. Global bauxite mines in 2007.—Continued

[km, kilometer; e, estimated; NA, not available]

Jamaica		
Jamaica Aluminum Company (Jamalco) (Alcoa World Alumina and Chemicals, 50%, and Government, 50%)	Bauxite mine, Manchester	NA
St. Ann Bauxite Company Ltd. (Falconbridge Ltd., 50%, and Century Aluminum Inc., 50%)	Bauxite mine, Discovery Bay[4]	4,500
West Indies Alumina Company (WINDALCO) (Glencore International AG, 93%, and Government, 7%)	Bauxite mine, Russell Place	NA
West Indies Alumina Company (WINDALCO) (Glencore International AG, 93%, and Government, 7%)	Bauxite mine in Schwallenburgh, Ewarton	NA
Kazakhstan		
Turgayskiy and Krasnooktyabrskiy bauxite mining complexes	Central Kazakhstan	5,000
Malaysia		
Johore Mining and Stevedoring Co. Sdn. Bhd. (Alcan Ltd. of Canada, 61%, and local investors and others, 39%)	Teluk Rumania, Johor Sg. Rengit, Johor	400
Montenegro		
Niksic Bauxite Mines (Central European Aluminum Co.)	Kutsko Brdo[2]	700
Mozambique		
E.C. Meikles (Pty) Ltd.	Monte Snuta[2]	e12
Romania		
Ministry of Industry	Oradea-Dobresti Mining Complex, near Hungarian border	350
Russia		
Komi Aluminum (SUAL Group)	Sredne-Timan	3,000
North-Urals mining company (SUAL Group)	Severoural'sk Region	NA
Severnaya Onega Mine (RUSAL)	Severnaya Onega Mine, Northwest Region	800
South-Urals mining company (SUAL Group)	South Ural Mountains	NA
Sierra Leone		
Sierra Mineral Holdings I Ltd. (Titanium Resources Group Ltd.)	SML Mine, 150 kilometers southeast of Freetown	1,200
Suriname		
Suriname Aluminum Co. (Suralco) (Alcoa, Inc., 55%, and BHP Billiton Ltd., 45%)	Kaaimangrasie Mine, open pit mine, located 38 kilometers southeast of Paramaribo (operations started in July 2006)[2]	2,000
Suralco	Klaverblad Mine, open pit mine, 23 kilometers southeast of Paramaribo (to commence in May 2007)[2]	2,000
Turkey		
Albuck Madencilik San. ve Tic. A.Ş.	Mine near Çırpı, Muğla Province	NA
Albuck Madencilik San. ve Tic. A.Ş.	Mine near Mihalıççık, Eskişehir Province	NA
Eti Alüminyum A.Ş. (Cengiz Holding)	Mines near Madenli, which is located about 25 kilometers south of Seydişehir, Konya Province	500
Venezuela		
C.V.G. Bauxilum C.A. (Corporación Venezolana de Guayana, 100%)	Los Pijiguaos, Bolivar State[2]	6,000

[1]In thousand metric tons per year.　　　　[2]Data are for 2008.

[3]Data are for 2009.　　　　[4]Combined capacity for Ewarton and Kirkvine.

Appendix 2.   Global alumina refineries in 2007.

[Unless otherwise noted, locations are for alumina. e, estimated; km, kilometer; NA, not available]

Major operating company	Location	Annual capacity[1]
Australia		
Gladstone alumina refinery [Queensland Alumina Ltd., operator (Rio Tinto Alcan, 80%, and Rusal, 20%)]	Gladstone, Queensland[2]	3,850
Gove alumina refinery [Alcan Gove Pty Ltd. (Rio Tinto Alcan, 100%)]	Nhulunbuy, Gove, Northern Territory[2]	3,800
Kwinana alumina refinery (Alcoa World Alumina Australia, 100%)	Kwinana, Western Australia[2]	2,100
Pinjarra alumina refinery (Alcoa World Alumina Australia, 100%)	Pinjarra, Western Australia[2]	4,200
Treibacher Schleifmittel AG	Plant at Villach[3]	100
Wagerup alumina refinery (Alcoa World Alumina Australia, 60%, and Western Mining Corp., 40%)	Waroona, Western Australia[2]	2,600
Worsley alumina refinery [Worsley Alumina Pty. Ltd., manager (BHP Billiton Ltd., 86%, and Japan Alumina Associates (Australia) Pty Ltd., 10%]	20 km northwest of Collie, Western Australia[2]	3,700
Yarwun alumina refinery (Rio Tinto Alcan, 100%)	Gladstone, Queensland[2]	1,400
Azerbaijan		
Gyandzha refinery	Ganca	100
Bosnia and Herzegovina		
Aluminij d.d. Mostar	Plant at Mostar	280
Ukio Banco Investment Group	Plants at Birac-Zvornik	600
Brazil		
Alcan Alumínio do Brasil S.A. [Alcan Aluminum Ltd., 100%]	Saramenha, Minas Gerais State (smelter and refinery)	150
Alumar Consortium S.A. (Alcoa Inc., 54%; BHP Billiton, 36%; Alcan Aluminum Ltd., 10%)	Sao Luis, Maranhao State (refinery)[4]	3,500
Alumínio do Norte do Brasil S.A. (Alunorte) (Vale S.A., 80%, and Norsk Hydro Comercio e Industria, 20%)	Barcarena, Para State (refinery)	7,400
Companhia Brasileira de Alumínio (CBA) (Votorantim Group, 100%)	Sorocaba, Sao Paulo State (refinery)	500
Companhia Geral do Minas (Aluminum Co. of America, 79%, and others, 21%)	Pocos de Caldas, Minas Gerais State (refinery)	275
Consortium Paragominas S.A. [Vale S.A., 48.7%; Mineração Rio do Norte S.A. (MRN), 24.6%; Nippon Amazon Aluminum Co., 12.2%; Companhia Brasileira de Alumínio (CBA), 5.7%; others, 8.8%]	Jabuti, Para State (alumina)	1,200
Canada		
Rio Tinto Alcan (Rio Tinto Group, 100%)	Refinery in Vaudreuil, Quebec[5]	55
Rio Tinto Alcan	Refinery in Vaudreuil, Quebec[5]	18
Rio Tinto Alcan	Refinery in Vaudreuil, Quebec[6]	1,300

Appendix 2. Global alumina refineries in 2007.—Continued

[Unless otherwise noted, locations are for alumina. e, estimated; km, kilometer; NA, not available]

China		
Bingzhou Weiqiao Aluminum Co.	Shandong, Zouping[7]	1,600
Chongqing Dingtai Tuoyuan Alumina Co.	Chongqing[7]	150
East Hope (Sanmenxia) Aluminum Co. Ltd.	Henan, Sanmenxia[4]	2,100
Guanxiangxia Aluminum Co. Ltd.	Hebei, Yicheng[7]	200
Guizhou Aluminum Plant [Aluminum Corporation of China (Chinalco)]	Guizhou, Guiyang[7]	1,200
Luoyang Wanji Xiangjiang Aluminum Co. Ltd.	Henan, Luoyang[7]	800
Nanchuan Pioneer Alumina Co.	Chongqing[7]	200
Pingdingshan Huiyuan Chemical Co.	Henan, Pingdingshan[7]	300
Pingguo Aluminum Co. [Aluminum Corporation of China (Chinalco)]	Guangxi, Pingguo[7]	1,200
Shandong Aluminum Plant [Aluminum Corporation of China (Chinalco)]	Shandong, Zibo	1,500
Shandong Huayu Alumina Co. Ltd. (Shandong Chiping Xinfa Aluminum and Electricity Group)	Shandong, Chiping[7]	1,800
Shanxi Aluminum Plant [Aluminum Corporation of China (Chinalco)]	Shanxi, Hejin[6]	2,200
Shanxi Luneng Jinbei Aluminum Co. Ltd.	Shanxi, Yuanping[7]	1,000
Yangquan Coalmine Aluminum (Sanmenxia) Co. Ltd.	Henan, Sanmenxia[4]	1,600
Yixiang Aluminum Co. (Henan Yima Coal Group)	Henan, Mainchi[7]	600
Zhengzhou Aluminum Plant [Aluminum Corporation of China (Chinalco)]	Hunan, Zhongzhou[7]	2,600
Zhongzhou Aluminum Plant [Aluminum Corporation of China (Chinalco)]	Hunan, Zhongzhou[7]	3,000
France		
Aluminium Pechiney (Alcan Inc., 97.95%)	Plant at Gardanne[8]	200
Germany		
Almatis GmbH (Dubai International Capital LLC)	Plant at Ludwigshafen	NA
Aluminium Oxid Stade GmbH (DADCO Alumina & Chemicals Ltd., 100%)	Plant at Stade	e1,000
Martinswerk GmbH (Albemarle Corporation, 100%)	Plant at Bergheim	350
Nabaltec GmbH	Plant at Schwandorf	120
Greece		
Aluminium de Grèce S.A. (AdG) (Mytilineos Holdings S.A., 53%)	Agios Nikolaos, Voiotia	750
Guinea		
Alumina Company of Guinea (United Company RUSAL, 100%)	Friguia plan, Fria	640
Hungary		
Magyar Aluminium Ltd. (MAL)	Ajka Timfoldgyar plant, about 120 km southwest of Budapest, near Lake Balaton	400
MAL	Almasfuzito Timfoldgyar plant near the Czech Republic border, 63 km northwest of Budapest	240
MAL	Moson-Magyarovar plant, in northwestern corner of Hungary, about 12 km from Austrian and Czech Republic borders	30

Appendix 2. Global alumina refineries in 2007.—Continued

[Unless otherwise noted, locations are for alumina. e, estimated; km, kilometer; NA, not available]

	India	
Bharat Aluminium Co. Ltd. (Indian Government, 49%, and Sterlite Industries Ltd., 51%)	Korba Refinery, Chhattisgarh	200
Hindalco Industries Ltd. (Birla Group, 33%; foreign investors, 26%; private Indian investors, 23%; financial institutions, 18%)	Renukoot Refinery, Uttar Pradesh	450
Indian Aluminium Co. Ltd. [Indian interests, 60.4%, and Alcan Aluminium Ltd. (Canada), 39.6%]	Belgaum Refinery, Karnataka[4]	350
Indian Aluminium Co. Ltd. [Indian interests, 60.4%, and Alcan Aluminium Ltd. (Canada), 39.6%]	Muri Refinery, Jharkhand[7]	450
Madras Aluminium Co. Ltd. (Sterlite Industries Ltd., 80%, and others, 20%)	Mettur Refinery, Tamil Nadu	80
National Aluminium Co. Ltd. (Indian Government, 100%)	Dhamanjodi Refinery, Orissa[4]	2,100
Utkal Alumina International Ltd. (Hindalco Industries Ltd., 100%)	Koraput Refinery, Orissa	1,500
	Iran	
Iran Alumina Co. (Government)	About 15 km northeast of Jajarm	280
	Ireland	
Aughinish Alumina plc (Glencore International AG)	Aughinish Island, County Limerick	1,500
	Italy	
Eurallumina S.p.A. (UC Rusal, 56.2%)	Plant at Portoscuso, Sardinia	1,000
	Jamaica	
Alumina Partners of Jamaica (ALPART) (Kaiser Aluminum Corp., 65%, and Hydro Aluminium Jamaica, 35%)	Refinery, Nain, St. Elizabeth[4]	1,700
Jamaica Aluminum Company (Jamalco) (Alcoa World Alumina and Chemicals, 50%, and Government, 50%)	Refinery at Halse Hall, Clarendon, 70 km west of Kingston[4]	2,240
West Indies Alumina Company (WINDALCO) (Glencore International AG, 93%, and Government, 7%)	Kirkvine Works refinery, Manchester	625
West Indies Alumina Company (WINDALCO) (Glencore International AG, 93%, and Government, 7%)	Ewarton Works refinery, Saint Catherine[9]	600
	Kazakhstan	
Pavlodar aluminum plant [Eurasian Nautral Resources Corp. (ENRC)]	Pavlodar	1,250
	Montenegro	
Kombinat Aluminijuma Podgorica (KAP) (Central European Aluminum Co., 59%)	Podgorica[6]	280
	Romania	
Alum S.A. (99.4% controlled, directly or indirectly, by Vimetco NV)	Plant at Tulcea, Danube Delta	500
Cemtrade Oradea (Part of CEAC Group)	Plant at Oradea, near Hungarian border	250
	Russia	
Achinsk (RUSAL)	Plant at Achinsk	900
Bogoslovsk (SUAL Group)	Bogolovsk aluminum smelter	1,050
Boksitogorsk (RUSAL)	Boksitogorsk plant	200
Pikalyovo (SUAL Group)	Pikalyovo plant[10]	300
Uralsk (SUAL Group)	Uralsk plant[7]	1,000

Appendix 2. Global alumina refineries in 2007.—Continued

[Unless otherwise noted, locations are for alumina. e, estimated; km, kilometer; NA, not available]

Spain		
Aluminio/Alúmina Española S.A. (Alcoa Inc., 60%, and Alumina Ltd., 40%)	Alumina plant at San Ciprian, Lugo[7]	1,500
Suriname		
Suriname Aluminum Co. (Suralco) (Alcoa, Inc., 55%, and BHP Billiton Ltd., 45%)	Refinery at Paranam, producing metallurgical-grade alumina[7]	2,200
Turkey		
Eti Alüminyum A.Ş. (Cengiz Holding)	Refinery at Seydişehir, Konya Province	200
Ukraine		
Mykolayiv refinery	Mykolayivs'ka Oblast'[4]	1,700
Zaporozh'ye (Dneprovsk) refinery	Zaporiz'ka Oblast'	245
United States		
Alcoa, Inc.	Point Comfort, Tex.	2,300
Noranda Aluminum	Gramercy, La.	1,250
Ormet Corp.	Burnside, La.	600
Sherwin Alumina (Glencore International)	Corpus Christi, Tex.	1,600
Venezuela		
C.V.G. Bauxilum C.A. (Corporación Venezolana de Guayana)	Ciudad Guayana, Bolivar State4	2,000

[1]In thousand metric tons per year.   [2]Alumina refinery.   [3]Fused alumina.   [4]Data are for 2009.

[5]Specialty-grade alumina.   [6]Smelter-grade alumina.   [7]Data are for 2008.   [8]Metallurgical alumina.

[9]Capacity in thousand dry metric tons per year.   [10]Permanently closed in 2008.

Appendix 3. Global aluminum smelters in 2007.

[Unless otherwise noted, locations are for aluminum. e, estimated; km, kilometer; NA, not available]

Major operating company	Location	Annual capacity[1]
Argentina		
Aluar Aluminio Argentino S.A.I.C. (private, 100%)	Abasto, Buenos Aires Province[2] Puerto Madryn, Chubut Province[2]	460
Australia		
Bell Bay aluminum smelter (Rio Tinto Alcan, 100%)	Bell Bay, Tasmania	160
Boyne Island aluminum smelter [Boyne Smelters Ltd., operator (Rio Tinto Alcan, 64%; Sumitomo Light Metal Industries Ltd., 17%; Ryowa Development Pty. Ltd., 12%; Kobe Steel Ltd., 5%; Sumitomo Chemical Co. Ltd., 2%)	Boyne Island, Queensland	550
Kurri Kurri aluminum smelter (Hydro Aluminium Kurri Kurri Pty. Ltd., 100%)	Kurri Kurri, near Newcastle, New South Wales	165
Point Henry aluminum smelter (Alcoa of Australia, 100%)	Point Henry, Victoria[2]	225
Portland aluminum smelter [Alcoa of Australia, 55%, manager; China International Trust Investment Co. (China's state-owned company), 22.5%; Marubeni Australia Pty. Ltd., 22.5%]	Portland, Victoria[2]	388
Tomago aluminum smelter [Tomago Aluminium Co. Pty. Ltd., operator (Gove Aluminium Finance Ltd., 36.05%; Rio Tinto Alcan, 51.55%; Hydro Aluminium, 12.40%)]	Tomago, New South Wales	525
Azerbaijan		
Sumgait smelter	Sumqayit	60
Bahrain		
Aluminium Bahrain B.S.C. (Alba) (Bahrain Mumtalakat Holding Co., 77%; SABIC Industrial Investments, 20%; Breton Investments, 3%)	Sitra (primary and secondary)	850
Bosnia and Herzegovina		
Aluminij d.d. Mostar	Smelter at Mostar	150
Brazil		
Albras-Alumínio Brasileiro S.A. (Albras) [Vale S.A., 51%, and Nippon Amazon Aluminio Co. (NAAC), 49%]	Vila do Conde, Para State (smelter) Belém, Para State (smelter)	455
Alcan Alumínio do Brasil S.A. [Alcan Aluminum Ltd., 100%]	Saramenha, Minas Gerais State (smelter and refinery)	100
Alcan Empreendimentos Ltda. (Alcan Alumínio do Brasil S.A., 100%)	Lamininacao de Pindamonhangaba, Sao Paulo State (smelter)	280
Alcoa Alumínio S.A. (Alcoa Inc., 54%; BHP Billiton, 36%; Alcan Aluminum Ltd., 10%)	Sao Luiz, Maranhao State (smelter)	239
Alumar Consortium S.A. (Alcoa Inc., 53.66%; BHP Billiton, 46.34%)	Sao Luis, Maranhao State (smelter)	1,000
Alumínio do Brasil Nordeste S.A. (Alcan Aluminum Ltd., 100%)	Aratu, Bahia State (smelter)	120
Companhia Brasileira de Alumínio (CBA) (Votorantim Group, 100%)	Sorocaba, Sao Paulo State (smelter)	400
Companhia Geral do Minas (Aluminum Co. of America, 79%, and others, 21%)	Pocos de Caldas, Minas Gerais State (smelter)	95
Aluvale (Vale S.A., 100%)	Santa Cruz, Rio de Janeiro State (smelter)	95
Cameroon		
Compagnie Camérounaise de l'Aluminium (Alcan Inc., 46.7%)	Plant at Edea	95

Appendix 3. Global aluminum smelters in 2007.—Continued

[Unless otherwise noted, locations are for aluminum. e, estimated; km, kilometer; NA, not available]

Canada		
Alcoa Ltd. (Alcoa Inc., 100%)	Smelter in Baie-Comeau, Quebec	438
Aluminerie Alouette Inc. (Rio Tinto Alcan, 40%; Aluminium Austria Metall Québec, 20%; Hydro Aluminum, 20%; Société générale de financement du Québec, 13.33%; Marubeni Québec Inc., 6.67%)	Smelter in Sept-Iles, Quebec	572
Aluminerie Lauralco Inc. (Alcoa Inc., 100%)	Deschambault, Quebec	254
Aluminiere de Bécancour Inc. (Alcoa Inc., 75%, and Rio Tinto Alcan, 25%)	Smelter in Becancour, Quebec	407
Rio Tinto Alcan (Rio Tinto Group, 100%)	Smelter in Alma, Quebec	415
Rio Tinto Alcan (Rio Tinto Group, 100%)	Smelter in Arvida, Jonquiere, Quebec	166
Rio Tinto Alcan (Rio Tinto Group, 100%)	Smelter in Beauharnois, Quebec[3]	52
Rio Tinto Alcan (Rio Tinto Group, 100%)	Smelter in Grande-Baie, Quebec	207
Rio Tinto Alcan (Rio Tinto Group, 100%)	Smelter in Kitimat, British Columbia	277
Rio Tinto Alcan (Rio Tinto Group, 100%)	Smelter in Laterriere, Quebec	228
Rio Tinto Alcan (Rio Tinto Group, 100%)	Smelter in Shawinigan, Quebec	99
China		
Baiyin Aluminum Plant	Gansu, Baiyin	150
Baotou Aluminum Plant	Nei Mongol, Baotou	250
Bingzhou Weiqiao Aluminum Co.	Shandong, Zouping	250
Chalco Zunyi Aluminum Co. Ltd.	Guizhou, Zunyi	130
East Hope Aluminum Plant	Nei Mongol, Baotou	330
Fushun Aluminum Plant	Liaoning, Fushun	190
Guizhou Aluminum Plant [Aluminum Corporation of China (Chinalco)]	Guizhou, Guiyang	400
Hanjiang Danjiangkou Aluminum Co. Ltd.	Hubei, Danjiangkou	110
Henan Shenhuo Aluminum-Electricity Co. Ltd.	Henan, Yongcheng	200
Henan Wanji Aluminum Co. Ltd.	Henan, Luoyang	180
Henan Zhongfu Industry Co. Ltd.	Henan, Gongyi	180
Henan Zhongmai Mianchi Aluminum Plant	Henan, Mianchi	400
Huaze Aluminum and Power Co. Ltd.	Shanxi, Hejin	400
Hunan Chuanquan Aluminum Co. Ltd.	Hunan, Taoyuan	210
Jiaozuo Wanfang Aluminum Co. Ltd.	Henan, Jiaozuo	420
Lanzhou Aluminum Plant	Gansu, Lanzhou	210
Liancheng Aluminum Plant	Gansu, Lanzhou	235
New Orient Aluminum Co. Ltd.	Shanxi, Taiyuan	75
Pingguo Aluminum Co. (Chinalco)	Guangxi, Pingguo	380
Qiaotou Aluminum Co. Electrolysis Branch	Qinghai, Datong	350
Qinghai Aluminum Smelter (Chinalco)	Qinghai, Xining	560
Qinghai West Mining Baihe Aluminum Co. Ltd.	Qinghai, Xining	112
Qingtongxia Aluminum Plant	Ningxia, Qingtongxia	580
Sanmenxia Tianyuan Aluminum Co. Ltd.	Henan, Sanmenxia	110
Shandong Aluminum Plant (Chinalco)	Shandong, Zibo	120
Shandong Chiping Xinfa Aluminum and Power Group	Shandong, Chiping	360
Shandong Nanshan Industry Co. Ltd.	Shandong, Longkou	280
Shangqiu Aluminum Smelter	Henan, Shangqiu	180
Shanxi Guanlu Aluminum Co. Ltd.	Shanxi, Yuncheng	210
Taishan Aluminum-Power Co. Ltd.	Shandong, Fecheng	125

Appendix 3. Global aluminum smelters in 2007.—Continued

[Unless otherwise noted, locations are for aluminum. e, estimated; km, kilometer; NA, not available]

China—Continued		
Tongchuan Xingguang Aluminum Co. Ltd.	Shaanxi, Tongchuan	250
Yichuan Yugang Longquan Aluminum Co.	Henan, Yichuan	600
Yinhai Aluminum Co. Ltd.	Guangxi, Laibin	125
Yunnan Aluminum Plant	Yunnan, Kunming	500
Zhengzhou Aluminum Plant (Chinalco)	Henan, Zhengzhou	60
Zouping Aluminum Co. Ltd.	Shandong, Zouping	150
Egypt		
Aluminium Co. of Egypt (Egyptalum) (Government, 80%, and private interests, 20%)	Nag Hammadi	230
France		
Aluminium Dunkerque (Alcan Inc., 97.95%)	Dunkerque, Calais du Nord	250
Aluminium Pechiney (Alcan Inc., 97.95%)	Saint-Jean-de-Maurienne, Savoie Province	120
Aluminium Pechiney	Nogueres, Pyrenees, Atlantiques Province	115
Aluminium Pechiney	Lannemezan, Hautes-Pyrenees Province[4]	63
Aluminium Pechiney	Auzat, Arieege Province (closed)	50
Germany		
Aluminium Norf GmbH [Novelis Inc. (Hindalco Industries Ltd., 100%), 50%, and Hydro Aluminium Deutschland GmbH, 50%]	Lippenwerk at Lünen (secondary)	1,500
Corus Aluminium Voerde GmbH (Tata Steel Ltd., 100%)	Primary smelter at Voerde, North Rhine-Westphalia	90
Hamburger Aluminium-Werk GmbH (HAW) (Trimet Aluminium AG, 100%)	Primary smelter at Hamburg	133
Hydro Aluminium Deutschland GmbH (Norsk Hydro ASA, 100%)	Rheinwerk primary smelter at Neuss	230
Trimet Aluminium AG	Smelter at Essen-Borbeck	175
Ghana		
Volta Aluminum Co. Ltd. (Valco) (Government, 90%, and Alcoa Inc., 10%)	Aluminum smelter at Tema	200
Greece		
Aluminium de Grèce S.A. (AdG) (Mytilineos Holdings S.A., 53%)	Agios Nikolaos, Voiotia	160
Hungary		
INOTAL Aluminium Processing Ltd.	Inota plant, near Varpalota, 75 km southwest of Budapest (primary)[5]	35
Iceland		
Century Aluminum Co.	Grundartangi	260
Icelandic Aluminium [ISAL], (Alusuisse-Lonza Holding Ltd., 100%)	Straumsvik	162
India		
Bharat Aluminium Co. Ltd. (Indian Government, 49%, and Sterlite Industries Ltd., 51%)	Korba Smelters, Chhattisgarh	350
Hindalco Industries Ltd. (Birla Group, 33%; foreign investors, 26%; private Indian investors, 23%; financial institutions, 18%)	Hirakud Smelter, Orissa[6]	155
Hindalco Industries Ltd.	Renukoot Smelter, Uttar Pradesh[2]	345
Indian Aluminium Co. Ltd. [Indian interests, 60.4%, and Alcan Aluminium Ltd. (Canada), 39.6%]	Alupuram Smelter, Kerala	20
Indian Aluminium Co. Ltd.	Belgaum Smelter, Karnataka	70
Madras Aluminium Co. Ltd. (Sterlite Industries Ltd., 80%, and others, 20%)	Mettur Smelter, Tamil Nadu	40
National Aluminium Co. Ltd. (Indian Government, 100%)	Angul Smelter, Orissa[6]	460

[Unless otherwise noted, locations are for aluminum. e, estimated; km, kilometer; NA, not available]

Indonesia		
PT Indonesia Asahan Aluminum (Nippon Asahan Aluminum Co. Ltd., 59%, and Government, 41%)	Kual Tanjun, North Sumatra	250
Iran		
Almahdi Aluminium Corp. [Iranian Mines and Mining Industries Development and Renovation Organization (IMIDRO),3 59.34%, and International Development Corp., 20.78%]	Bandar Abbas[2]	260
Iran Aluminium Co. [Iranian Mines and Mining Development and Renovation Organization (IMIDRO)]	Arak	155
Italy		
Alcoa Italia S.p.A.	Smelters at Fusina, near Venice	44
Alcoa Italia S.p.A. (Alcoa Inc., 100%)	Smelters at Porto Vesme, Sardinia	159
Montenegro		
Kombinat Aluminijuma Podgorica (KAP) (Central European Aluminum Co., 59%)	Podgorica (primary)	120
Mozambique		
Mozambique Aluminum SARL (BHP Billiton Ltd., 47%)	Mozal smelter at Beluluane	563
Netherlands		
Corus Group	Smelter at Delfzijl (primary)	100
Pechiney Nederland NV (Alcan Inc., 85%)	Plant at Flushing (Vlissingen) (primary)	230
Pechiney Nederland NV (Alcan Inc., 85%)	Plant at Flushing (Vlissingen) (billet)	213
New Zealand		
Tiwai Point smelter [New Zealand Aluminium Smelters Ltd. (Rio Tinto Alcan, 79.36%, and Sumitomo Chemical Co., 20.64%)]	Southland, Invercargill	350
Nigeria		
Aluminum Smelter Co. of Nigeria, Ltd. (ALSCON) (United Company RUSAL, 77.5%)	Smelter at Ikot Abasi[7]	193
Norway		
Elkem Aluminium ANS (Elkem A/S, 50%, and Alcoa Inc., 50%)	Smelter at Farsund (Lista)[8]	96
Elkem Aluminium ANS (Elkem A/S, 50%, and Alcoa Inc., 50%)	Smelter at Mosjoen[8]	190
Hydro Aluminium ANS (Norsk Hydro A/S, 70%)	Plant at Holmestrand[8]	176
Hydro Aluminium ANS (Norsk Hydro A/S, 70%)	Smelter at Ardal[8]	233
Hydro Aluminium ANS (Norsk Hydro A/S, 70%)	Smelter at Hoyanger[8]	60
Hydro Aluminium ANS (Norsk Hydro A/S, 70%)	Smelter at Karmoy[8]	290
Hydro Aluminium ANS (Norsk Hydro A/S, 70%)	Smelter at Sunndal[8]	360
Sor-Norge Aluminium A/S (Alusuisse Group, 50%, and Hydro Aluminium ANS, 49%)	Smelter at Odda	50
Poland		
Aluminum Konin-Impexmetal S.A.	Smelter at Konin (primary)	55
Romania		
Alro S.A. (87% controlled, directly or indirectly, by Vimetco NV)	Slatina, 120 km west of Bucharest (primary)	300

Appendix 3. Global aluminum smelters in 2007.—Continued

[Unless otherwise noted, locations are for aluminum. e, estimated; km, kilometer; NA, not available]

	Russia	
Bogoslovsk (SUAL Group)	Bogoslovsky plant (primary)[2]	190
Bratsk (RUSAL)	Bratsk plant (primary)	950
Irkutsk (SUAL Group)	Irkutsk plant (primary)[2]	460
Kandalaksha (SUAL Group)	Kandalaksha plant (primary)	75
Khakaz (RUSAL)	Khakaz plant (primary)[2]	370
Krasnoyarsk (RUSAL)	Krasnoyarskiy plant (primary)[2]	1,000
Nadvoitsy (SUAL Group)	Nadvoitsy plant (primary)	75
Novokuznetsk (RUSAL)	Novokuznetsk plant (primary)[2]	330
Sayansk (RUSAL)	Sayansk plant (primary)[2]	520
Uralsk (SUAL Group)	Uralsk plant (primary)	150
Volgograd (SUAL Group)	Volgograd plant (primary)	175
Volkhov (SUAL Group)	Volkhov plant (primary)	20
	Slovakia	
ZSNP Aluminum Works (Slovalco a.s.)	Ziar, Central Slovakia	195
	Slovenia	
Talum d.d. Kidričevo	Smelter at Kidricevo	120
	South Africa	
BHP Billiton Ltd.	Bayside smelter at Richards Bay	180
BHP Billiton Ltd.	Hillside smelter at Richards Bay	700
	Spain	
Alcoa Inespal S.A. (Alcoa Inc., 100%	Electrolytic plant at Aviles	93
Alcoa Inespal S.A. (Alcoa Inc., 100%)	Electorlytic plant at La Coruña	87
Aluminio/Alúmina Española S.A. (Alcoa Inc., 60%, and Alumina Ltd., 40%)	Electrolytic plant at San Ciprian, Lugo	228
	Sweden	
Granges AB (Glencore International AG, 100%)	Sundsvall smelter at Kubikenborg	100
	Switzerland	
Novelis Inc. (Hindalco Industries Ltd., 100%)	Plant at Sierre[9]	168
	Tajikistan	
Tajik aluminum plant (TadAZ)	Tursunzade	517
	Turkey	
Eti Alüminyum A.Ş. (Cengiz Holding)	Smelter at Seydişehir, Konya Province	65
	Ukraine	
Zaporozh'ye (Dneprovsk) smelter	Zaporiz'ka Oblast' (primary)	120
	United Arab Emirates	
Dubai Aluminum Company Ltd. (Investment Corporation of Dubai, 100%)	Jebel Ali, Dubai	950
	United Kingdom	
Anglesey Aluminium Metal Ltd. (Rio Tinto Corp., 51%, and Kaiser Aluminum and Chemical Corp., 49%)	Holyhead, Gwynedd, Wales (primary)[3]	144
British Alcan Aluminium Ltd.	Locchaber Smelter, Fort William, Scotland (primary)	41
British Alcan Aluminium Ltd.	Lynemouth Smelter, Northumberland, England (primary)	169

Appendix 3. Global aluminum smelters in 2007.—Continued

[Unless otherwise noted, locations are for aluminum. e, estimated; km, kilometer; NA, not available]

United States		
Alcoa	Alcoa, Tenn. (primary)	215
Alcoa	Evansville, Ind. (primary)	309
Alcoa	Ferndale, Wash. (primary)	278
Alcoa	Massena (east), N.Y. (primary)	130
Alcoa	Massena (St. Lawrence), N.Y. (primary)	125
Alcoa	Rockdale, Tex. (primary)	267
Alcoa	Wenatchee, Wash. (primary)	184
Alcoa/Century	Mount Holly, S.C. (primary)	224
Century Aluminum	Hawesville, Ky. (primary)	244
Century Aluminum	Ravenswood, W. Va. (primary)	170
Glencore	Columbia Falls, Mt. (primary)	168
Noranda	New Madrid, Mo. (primary)	250
Ormet	Hannibal, Ohio (primary)	265
Rio Tinto Alcan	Sebree, Ky. (primary)	196
Venezuela		
C.V.G. Aluminio del Caroní, S.A. (Corporación Venezolana de Guayana and others)	Ciudad Guayana, Bolivar State	210
C.V.G. Venezolana de Aluminio C.A. (Corporación Venezolana de Guayana, 80%, and Showa Denko K.K., Kobe Steel Ltd., Sumitomo Chemical Co. Ltd., Mitsubishi Materials Corp., Mitsubishi Aluminum Co., and Marubeni Corp., 20%)	Ciudad Guayana, Bolivar State	430

[1]In thousand metric tons per year.   [2]Data are for 2009.   [3]Permanently closed in 2009.

[4]Permanently closed in 2008.   [5]Closed.   [6]Data are for 2008.   [7]Under rehabilitation.

[8]Soderberg pots closed.   [9]Permanently closed in 2006.